Documentary as Autoethnography

A Case Study Based on the Changing Surnames of Women

Hande Çayır

Series in Anthropology

VERNON PRESS

In the Americas:	In the rest of the world:
Vernon Press	Vernon Press
1000 N West Street,	C/Sancti Espiritu 17,
Suite 1200, Wilmington,	Malaga, 29006
Delaware 19801	Spain
United States	

Series in Anthropology

Library of Congress Control Number: 2020935122

ISBN: 978-1-64889-071-0

Also available: 978-1-62273-759-8 [Hardback]; 978-1-64889-009-3 [PDF, E-Book]

Cover design by Vernon Press. Cover photography by Ege Kanar.

*This research is dedicated to Mickey
and
to my partner, Mehmet, who has been a
constant source
of support and encouragement*

Table of Contents

Acknowledgements

I would like to thank the academic professionals and my loved ones who have assisted me through this research project. In particular:

To my early MA supervisor, Nurşen Bakır, who encouraged me to shoot my documentary, chatted with me and showed a keen interest whenever I needed, gave me loads of chocolates, and supported me when I doubted myself; through her I found my balance. I am very lucky to know her, and to be her student.

To my principal supervisor, Feride Çiçekoğlu, for her theoretical and practical evaluation at every stage of my PhD. She shared her wisdom and to-the-point anecdotes, and motivated me with invaluable critiques. I sincerely appreciated her life story and her works of art, especially Mickey from *Uçurtmayı Vurmasınlar / Don't Let Them Shoot the Kite* (1989), as this was where I learned about "becoming". She helped me to stay focused and lent her ear whenever necessary, which was very precious to me. Most importantly, she defined herself as my "journey-mate" and never abandoned me.

To the vivid ensemble of academic committee members, Aslı Tunç, Ayşegül Yaraman, Diğdem Sezen, and Itır Erhart, for all their constructive feedback. I am grateful that they were the ones who first read my research, and provided the appropriate environment for me to present my work with self-confidence.

To my dedicated editor and friend, Melissa Maples, for being around whenever I needed her.

To the brave women who have followed my work with a certain smile: Hande Varsat and Duygu Kürklü.

Most importantly, to the women in Amargi İstanbul, in Filmmor Women's Cooperative, in Purple Roof Women's Shelter Foundation, and all those in the global women's movement, who reminded me that I am not alone in this struggle.

I would also like to thank my dearest friend, A. Armağan Kilci, who helped me to maintain my authenticity, and who shared everything with me in emergencies: his food, his bed, and his heart.

I would like to express my gratitude to my mother, Yasemen Çayır.

Many thanks to my colleagues for their worthwhile inspiration, which grows in me day by day, from one researcher to another, thank you.

Preface:
From *Aydın* to *Çayır* and from "Yes" to "How?"

Feride Çiçekoğlu

When I first met Hande, her last name was Aydın, and she used the word "Yes" a lot. I remember her during a conversation after she was accepted to the master program in Film and Television at İstanbul Bilgi University: A contemplative young woman with an interesting portfolio who had an undergraduate degree in Visual Arts & Visual Communication Design from one of the best universities in Turkey. She made an impression on me as someone who was not quite sure what she was looking for. She answered most of my questions with a hesitant "yes", without giving many clues about her real motivation or what drove her to pursue graduate study in film and television.

Almost a decade after that conversation which took place in 2010, I now smile at myself for that past impression. It is a memory I try to rejuvenate every once in a while, especially during the time of interviews for new applications, so that I do not misjudge or I do not even judge anyone I meet for the first time without giving a second thought. If Hande had not been persistent to confide in me, I might have missed her. And what a loss it would be! Not that it was an easy journey, but the whole adventure was worth it: Hande has become a friend and a colleague, someone with whom I learned a lot as her doctorate dissertation supervisor so that I hope I became a better tutor and a better person.

Hande did not only change her last name from Aydın to Çayır and her status from married to single during the first two years that I knew her, but she also changed her vision and the way she spoke. Gradually "yes" ceased to be the most frequent word she used as she ceased avoiding eye contact, being lost in her own thoughts and ruminating over as if looking for an alternative way to respond rather than merely affirming. She started to look directly into my eyes while searching for answers as to how she could make her documentary better or how she could go on exploring herself in her further studies.

The documentary that she made as her master graduation project was a transformative experience, not only for her but also for those of us who were on her committee. The name of the documentary is *Mrs. His Name*, and the first shot is from a touristic trip in a Nordic country with her then-husband and his brother. While the husband is driving, with his brother in the front seat, Hande is at the back seat. She is bored and she asks for his phone since hers does not have a camera. She starts shooting from the back seat, asking questions to her husband. His answers make her quiet. She feels she is not understood. He says, "Hande! Hande!" and when she does not answer, he calls out "Hey!" We hear the voiceover of Hande saying she wants to make a documentary about the changing surname of women when they get married. The husband responds: "It has been an unnecessary project. It's meaningless. There are a lot of subjects to film, couldn't you find anything else? Do something worthwhile. Leave women's issues alone. Did you hear me? Am I talking to the wall? Hande? Give me an answer…" Hande is quiet then, but the film itself will turn out to be her answer.

In the end, the process of making the film became one of documenting how she drifted apart from her husband while asking questions about why she had lost her voice. There is a beautiful sequence in the film where she is experiencing to make sounds with the consonants, which fail to turn into words since the vowels are missing. Her film was a way of getting back her vowels, relearning to speak with her own words and regaining her self esteem. By the time she finished her documentary with her husband's surname, she had decided to get a divorce.

So here she was, faced with a change of the surname a second time, having to change all her paperwork, including all her identification documents such as her birth certificate, her driver's license and her passport. And she realised that she had somehow developed an alter ego or a second personality all the while when she was Aydın, and now she had to switch back to Çayır, which was not as easy as she had thought it would be. It was at this stage that we had a strong bond with Hande, and she decided to go on with her graduate studies by applying to our newly founded Communication Studies doctoral program.

When she wanted to work with me as her dissertation supervisor, this time I had no hesitations, although I had no idea how we would proceed methodologically. Hande had framed her research question for her doctoral dissertation proposal as an extension of her documentary: She wanted to research her own story and the making of her own film as a case study of how the change of surname affected women. We had long sessions of discussion, and in the end she discovered the method on her own.

I recall two events highlighting her search: The first was early in our collaborative journey, Hande beaming up when she announced that her paper *Autoethnography as Documentary: My Story is (Y)ours* was accepted for a conference – *Doing Autoethnography: (Re) Writing, Self, Other and Society –*

which was held in the United States in 2013. The second was when Hande discovered a soul mate in a PhD thesis from the other end of the world: *Be(com)ing Reel Independent Woman: An Autoethnographic Journey Through Female Subjectivity and Agency in Contemporary Cinema with Particular Reference to Independent Scriptwriting Practice.* It was the thesis of Larissa Sexton-Finck who came to our rescue all the way from Australia, bonding us stronger than ever since I had made my complicated journey back to academia via scriptwriting.

By the time Hande finished writing her dissertation with her birth surname – *Documentary as Autoethnography: A Case Study Based on the Changing Surnames of Women* – we had already won the battle that her method was a valid one for her field of research, having introduced autoethnography as a brand new idea to our brand new program. And by the time Hande had her degree as the first graduate of our program, she had not only regained her full voice but had started singing jazz tunes.

It is such a joy to write this introduction, knowing that I still accompany her at this new stage of her journey. When the second decade of the new century is about to reach closure, I look back and see that it has been the best one I remember in terms of the self-assertiveness and the visibility of women. So good to know our collaboration with Hande had a tiny contribution to the past decade and will hopefully continue to have even more so with each reader of this book during the next one.

Overview:
Surname Conventions Around the World

"What could be simpler to understand than the act of people representing what they know best, their own lives?". This is the question asked by Sidone Smith and Julia Watson in their article (2010, 1) "Life Narrative: Definitions and Distinctions". In this article, they referred to works including Glückel of Hameln's memoirs and Rousseau's confessions, exploring autobiography, memoir, life writing, and life narrative. I am sharing part of my story in this book, and as it has been my exploration of self, family, and the society I live in, it was difficult to give it a title. Smith and Watson (2010) emphasise that such a journey "can employ the dialogue, plot, setting, and density of language of the novel. It may incorporate biographies of others in its representation of family, friends, historical or religious figures. It projects multiple histories—of communities, families, nations, movements" (19). Therefore, this research includes the story of my surname changes after marriage and divorce, and details Turkey's naming conventions. However, before focusing on that, I would like to share some views around the world regarding this issue.

After completing the writing portion of this research in 2016, I met people all around the world and continued asking questions about their surname change stories. I want to mention some of them here in order to document the universality of this topic. For example, Stephanie Angela de Palma, 43, a filmmaker and part-time waitress from New Jersey, says that her name "has been Stephanie Angela De Palma McClelland and Stephanie Angela De Palma Cook and at some points even Stephanie Angela De Palma McClelland Cook". Stephanie Angela de Palma has been divorced twice, and notes that in the US, the surname change decision depends on the individual. "Honestly, if I got married again, I would keep my name as it is. It is just a hassle in my opinion. If you love somebody that is not really the way to prove it. I felt I lost my identity for a bit and I am happy to have back now", said de Palma. She has used many names on formal documents and it is incredibly confusing to government and banking institutions. She said that she often cannot be found in the system because parties cannot differentiate who she is. She has used different names for her bank account, passport, and UK Leave to Remain visa. In the end, she had to get a new passport, at her own personal expense.

Nicki Clayton, 55, an entrepreneur and hairstylist from the UK, says that "women can do whatever they want with their name: get married but keep their own surname, take their husband's name when getting married, return to their own name (called their 'maiden' name) once divorced. Also, anyone can change their name by deed poll (officially) if they want to assume another name."

Eshna Ramrekha, 24, an optometrist from Mauritius, says "Mauritius is still a developing country and some things are still backwards or considered as a tradition. When a woman gets married, she would change her surname to her husband's surname."

Su'ur Su'eddie Vershima Agema, 32, a poet and editor from Nigeria, says that usually when Nigerian women divorce, they file for a change of name in a court, supported by the divorce papers. Afterwards, they have it published in at least two national newspapers. "Most times they do not change their names in full because they have come to be known through that name. They have built reputations and careers with that name so they cannot abruptly just drop the name," said Agema. Most also end up adding in their father's name in a hyphenated form.

Eman Mohamed Magdy Tawfik Elharmeel, 32, a filmmaker from Egypt, says "generally, in Egypt, we have only one option which is keeping your family surname and it is not allowed legally to take your husband's surname. But you should mention your husband's name in your official ID after marriage such as national ID and passport."

Shuai Ma, 29, a student from China, says "generally speaking, Chinese surnames are handed down from ancient times, and children usually inherit their fathers' surnames. There are also a small number of children who follow their mother's surname. In modern China, women's surnames are not changed by marriage or divorce."

Nuno Juvenal Figueira Fernandes, 27, a data analyst from Portugal, says the following:

> "It has not always been this way. Today, both partners—husbands and spouses—can add, if s/he wants, two surnames at the most from the other partner. They can also keep their surnames. The same rule is not applied to whom already has surnames from a previous marriage. Surnames can be taken after the divorce, and at a court request, one partner can be deprived of using his former partner surname, if s/he feels prejudiced."

Fernandes added that "the answers do not reflect the 'cultural Portuguese mind', only what the law allows. Women keep getting their husbands names despite the possibility that they can choose not to."

Amanat Ali, 40, who is working with the government as a civil servant from Pakistan, says "there is no definitive pattern of the use of surnames in my country. Some people do like to use family name but others may not. Hence, there is no set pattern." That said, the majority of Pakistani women do change their surnames after marriage to the names of their husbands. Ali adds that "however, the practice is new. There are significant numbers of the ladies who do not change their surname despite the insistence of their husbands. The women belonging to old times would not change their surnames. The practice is getting currency only now."

Agnieszka Podubny, 33, a singer and singing teacher from Poland, says that she is saddened to see young Polish women sticking with the outdated and conservative practice of switching to the husband's surname. Her view is that most women think of it in terms of avoiding unnecessary arguments, or not wanting to hurt their husband's feelings.

I know just a few girls who have chosen to have two surnames; they are highly educated and successful in their career. I do not know any who keep only her surname after marriage. If I get married I would definitely keep my surname, I do not see the point why I should change it. Woman after divorce almost always return to their own surnames. On the other side I know one couple in which husband took a wife's name, probably because his own was a matter of jokes and both of the surnames when they come together sounded even more funny so they wanted to have things easier for their child's future.

Katie Barclay is a historian of marriage, and she says in *What's in a Name? Or Leaving Your Patrilineage Behind* (2010) that "in Iceland, things were different again, with women taking their mother's first name as a surname, and men taking their father's. So, I would be Katie Fionas daughter, while my brother would be Liam Billysson." (1) As can be seen from these examples, surname changes differ from culture to culture, but generally, the practice is male-dominant. Nevertheless, we should always look into the context before judging anyone's personal decision; this is what I learned from this research.

Over the years, I came across some women who wanted to change their surname to their husband's because they hated their father. Sometimes it is the other way around. Some simply enjoyed having a surname change. Sometimes mothers chose to do it solely for the sake of their children. Some gay couples made up their own surnames. One day a work colleague changed her surname and everybody celebrated, assuming she had married; however, we later realised that she had actually divorced. Surnames carry a message, as do our first names. I believe it should be one's own decision. If an institution (i.e. state) or someone other than you (i.e. your ex-partner) has a right to change even your name, then in what way are you still free? Or, are we private properties? Gabriele Rosenthal (1993) says in *Reconstruction of Life Stories: Principles of Selection in Generating Stories for Narrative Biographical Interviews* that "the present perspective determines what the subject considers biographically relevant, how he or she develops thematic and temporal links between his or her various experiences and how past, present or anticipated future realities influence his or her personal interpretation of the meaning of his or her life". (3) When it comes to theory, I would say it is easy to see the whole picture, but when it comes to practical life, I am not sure what to say. The meaning constantly changes depending on your perspective.

Introduction

I shall speak about women's writing: about what it will do. Woman must write herself: must write about women and bring women to writing, from which they have been driven away as violently as from their bodies—for the same reasons, by the same law, with the same fatal goal. Woman must put herself into text—as into the world and into history— by her own movement. (Cixous 1976, 875)

In 2008, when I was planning to write a statement of purpose for an MA degree application, one of my friends tentatively warned me—after witnessing my enthusiasm—that I could not study self in an academic context. In the impulse of the moment, I could not remember Meister Eckhart's well-known words that "a human being has so many skins inside, covering the depths of the heart. We know so many things, but we do not know ourselves" (Allen 2015, 33), or Jean La Fontaine's "He knows the universe and does not know himself" (Slater 2001, 164), or Yunus Emre's "Knowledge means to know yourself, heart and soul / If you have failed to understand yourself / Then all of your reading has missed its call" (Eryaman 2012, 59). In short, although I could not respond then, my friend's comment failed to convince me and triggered the momentum to delve into the subject.

In 2012, at the very beginning of my PhD journey in Communications, it all recurred in the same way. In the *Inquiry of Knowledge* course, we as students were tasked to discuss our prospective PhD theme, to select a methodology, and to contribute the factual and theoretical knowledge of communication discipline. Thankfully, I had already researched a topic while making my documentary and wanted to go further with it. For that reason, I wrote in my academic paper that I would like to research women's changing surnames in Turkey; as a starting point and case study, I would like to use my own personal experience. In the meantime, I questioned the aim of the scientific research: is it about knowing oneself better, or rather about knowing more about something outside the self?

After a while, some of my classmates abandoned their PhD paths for various reasons. The effects of dissimilar point of views through constructing reliable academic knowledge, which I will discuss later, initially made me feel like abandoning my own track as well. In those moments, I just needed to drive somewhere else in the universe, somewhere with fantastic, colourful lights, where I could get an entirely different perspective. Deep down, I wholeheartedly believed and had personal knowledge that the self can be studied in academia, since I had completed two oral history projects with the guidance of anthropologist and professor Leyla Neyzi while I was studying for my BA degree at Sabancı University in 2003. I had devoted myself on every level to those projects, in which we were taking field notes, adding our emotions in detail, and focusing on ourselves as researchers as well.

When frustration comes, my usual inclination is to head to the library. In this regard, I lost myself in books like *The Dance of Qualitative Research Design, Feminist Methods in Social Research* and *Real World Research.* After spending a huge amount of time with these publications, suddenly something beautiful happened: I came across a methodology called autoethnography. In an overview concerning the methodology, autoethnography was described as

[...] an approach to research and writing that seeks to describe and systematically analyse personal experience in order to understand cultural experience. This approach challenges canonical ways of doing research and representing others and treats research as a political, socially-just and socially-conscious act. A researcher uses tenets of autobiography and ethnography to do and write autoethnography. Thus, as a method, autoethnography is both process and product. (Ellis and Adams and Bochner 2011, 273)

From that point onward I researched autoethnography, joined autoethnographic online research groups, found international scholars who are professionals in the field, read numerous journals, and finally presented my research paper titled *Autoethnography as Documentary: My Story is (Y)ours,* at the Doing Autoethnography: (Re) Writing, Self, Other, and Society conference, which was held in the United States in 2013.[1] In the sessions, I had a chance to meet in person with dedicated autoethnographers such as Tami Spry, Tony E. Adams, and Stacy Holman Jones. Spry, for example, focuses on performative autoethnography in her work titled *Performing Autoethnography: an Embodied Methodological Praxis,* where she argues the personal, professional, and political potential of autoethnographic performance as a critical self-reflexive discourse (2001, 706). Similarly, Adams and Holman Jones focus on intersections of reflexivity as a writing practice in their article entitled "Telling

---

[1] Organised by Derek Bolen, the conference was held at San Angelo State University on 1 March 2013. The Doing Autoethnography conferences are organised annually by the same team each February-March; I participated in the second conference.

Stories: Reflexivity, Queer Theory, and Autoethnography" and write queer personal passages in order to question "challenges of open texts" and "to test the limits of knowledge and certainty" (2011, 108). Hence, after reading their work, I felt strong enough to defend my position.

During that period, our university's library acquired fundamental autoethnography books at the request of an emerging autoethnographer: me. In addition, surprisingly, I thought I found my soulmate, that is to say, a PhD thesis, called *Be(com)ing Reel Independent Woman: An Autoethnographic Journey Through Female Subjectivity and Agency in Contemporary Cinema with Particular Reference to Independent Scriptwriting Practice* by Larissa Sexton Finck. Immediately sharing this fruitful thesis with my prospective advisor, Feride Çiçekoğlu, who is also a scriptwriter among other things, assisted me in sensing and finding my path.

Choosing a research method is not a simple act for a PhD student, because personal position and values, legitimacy of the method, and the reliability of the research all have to be taken into account. Therefore, autoethnography allows me to frame my values within the academic setting. I conducted this research in the context of an interdisciplinary communications studies programme in which a variety of social science thinkers have contributed to the field. My panoramic research includes five fundamental chapters featuring surname changes, methodology, theory, documentary, and participatory culture.

The first chapter is about surname changes, mainly in Turkey. How do human beings experience the surname change issue in terms of the protection of equal legal, social, and economic rights? Bearing in mind the feminist quote "the personal is political" (Hanisch 1970, 1), I started my own research and found out that women in Turkey are required to change their surname when they marry and divorce. If they would like to continue using their ex-husband's surname after a divorce, they need to get permission from both the ex-husband and the state. Because of this unfair policy, some women have appealed to the European Court of Human Rights (ECHR). Furthermore, men have the right to take their surname back after a divorce. Did surname changes affect women financially? Have forced surname changes been a barrier for women's careers? This chapter will focus on the issue of surname changes through real cases in order to illustrate bell hooks' (2000) famous quote, "being oppressed means the absence of choices" (5).

The focus of the second chapter will be the method, autoethnography, where researchers analyse their own subjectivity and life experiences, and treat the self as "other" while "calling attention to issues of power" (Jupp 2006, 16). I will dig first-hand into its definition, history, potential research topics, data collection, and the idea of the researcher as a subject. As in autoethnography, "the researcher and the researched, the dominant and the subordinate, individual experience and socio-cultural structures" can be examined (Jupp 2006, 16). I will attempt to construct a dynamic framework through discussing the work of autoethnography pioneers such as Carolyn Ellis (in communication), Tony E. Adams (in queer studies), Stacy Holman Jones (in feminist and queer studies), Heewon Chang (in anthropology), Kip Jones (in film), Tami Spry and Norman K. Denzin (in performance studies), and Kim Etherington (in psychotherapy). The goal is to penetrate into the concrete details of life, and understand oneself in deeper ways. As "writing vulnerably, evocatively and ethically" (Ellis 2004, 119) is the core element—instead of dealing with hypotheses—in this research method (Ellis 2004, 3), the emphasis will be a process of slice-of-life discovery (Ellis 2004, 10) and vivid descriptions. (Ellis 2004, 60) I followed *Autoethnography as Method* (2008) by Chang, who refers to the four types of autoethnography as descriptive-realistic writing, confessional-emotive writing, analytical-interpretive writing, and imaginative-creative writing (139-151). By keeping those types in mind, I will also be investigating the method through questions: Why does someone want to study her or his own self? How will someone collect the data about the self? How will s/he manage the interpretation process? What will be the outcomes?

In the third chapter, my focus will be the theoretical framework, mainly depending on feminist theory, while viewing "the personal is political" and giving voice to "other". In the process, different aspects of feminist theory will be addressed in detail, thus forming a framework within which the research question of the present study can be assessed. This is, namely, whether the documentary based on the surname changes of the researcher at marriage and divorce can be taken as a case study, opening up our comprehension of women's surname changes as a human rights issue. In this regard, the interdisciplinary nature of this enquiry highlights the link between surnames and identity, which is a crucial human rights debate, while demonstrating the problem of "the gaze of the other" (Prasad 2003, 3). Moreover, theory in practice and practice in theory will go hand in hand, because this research contains a second component: my documentary *Yok Anasının Soyadı / Mrs His Name*[2] (2012), which demonstrates my exploration in surname changes via film (practice) and research (theory) on the same subject.

---

[2] The English title of the documentary was inspired by Jean M. Twenge's article (1997) "Mrs His Name: Women's Preferences for Married Names".

In the fourth chapter, I will discuss the power of documentaries, and specifically the impact of autoethnographic documentaries. As a case study and "practice-led research"[3] (Nimkulrat 2007, 1), I will present my filmmaking experience. The seventeen-minute documentary is defined as "a form of self-narrative that places the self within a social context" (Reed Danahay 1997, 9). Hence, "the cinema of me" (Lebow 2012, 1) has been transformed into collective expressions of identity. In the meantime, I will also try to unleash the autoethnographic filmmaking mechanisms in Chantal Akerman's *News from Home* (1977) and Zemirah Moffat's *Mirror Mirror* (2009), where the outputs are constructed with regard to social memory and identity. In these examples, documentary filmmakers choose whether to include their own voice into the film. Indeed, even from the outside, it is possible to interpret the final output in relation to the person who made the film. "The other" is not passive, not driven by an authority that is more reflexive and anarchic rather than obedient in autoethnographic films. Not only a personal identity, but also a cultural one can be generated in the process of production of this documentary form. In conclusion, I will share the autoethnographic films that can bring us closer to the human experience and assist in the process of change.

In the last chapter, I will strive to set a relationship between what I did in my documentary and the possible effects in the communications discipline, where the capacity of digital media has the power to change the political game. In other words, social media challenges traditional media, and increasing accessibility has made the internet a creative hub that connects people with others who have the same goals. I would like to highlight and conclude how the experience of "participatory culture"[4] hones the primary output, that is to say, my documentary's distribution and circulation[5] journey. In a networked

---

[3] In practice-led research, Nimkulrat (2007) shows that "documentation of art practice can be used as research material". (2)

[4] In *Confronting the Challenges of Participatory Culture: Media Education for the 21st Century*, Henry Jenkins (2009) and his colleagues demonstrate that participatory cultures are identified by "relatively low barriers to artistic expression and civic engagement, strong support for creating and sharing one's creations, and some type of information mentorship whereby what is known by the most experienced is passed along to novices. A participatory culture is also one in which members believe their contributions matter, and feel some degree of social connections with one another." (5)

[5] I completed my documentary in 2012 and wrote my thesis in 2016. Now, in 2020, the circulation journey of documentaries is a bit different than it was eight years ago. For example, we used to send out films via DVD to the proper addresses; nowadays we use online platforms such as FilmFreeway or ShortFilmDepot. In this way, we all experience a much more fast-paced distribution journey for films.

culture, we spread information via social media tools. For this purpose, by referring to participatory culture and its open-endedness, I would like to bring hope. As Jim Chambers says, "we can become more possible than they can powerfully imagine" (No M11 Link Road campaign) (Harding 2001, 1).

Chapter 1

Women's Surname Changes

1.1 Individual Experience Juxtaposes Cultural Structures

How do women experience the surname change issue in terms of the protection of equal, legal, social, and economic rights? I first started to think about this question in a larger context when my own surname was changed without my consent after my marriage in 2008. One day I realised I had two diplomas, each with a different name on it, even though both those people were me. Visually, my name had multiplied like an amoeba: Hande Çayır, Hande Aydın, Hande Çayır Aydın. From this visible sign, people around me—for example, the civil establishment—gained the apparent right to talk about my personal life in the public sphere.

Afterward, I remembered the feminist quote "the personal is political", started my own research, and found out that women in Turkey are required to change their surname when they marry and divorce. If they would like to continue using their ex-husband's surname after a divorce, they need to get permission from both the ex-husband and the state. Because of this unfair policy, some women appealed to the ECHR, and subsequently, the ECHR is requiring the Turkish government to pay an indemnity. Thus, the link between surnames and identity is a crucial human rights debate. The media portrays this issue as one that is currently being solved. However, after my visit to the Grand National Assembly of Turkey, I came to the conclusion that the process is not moving forward at all.

The first time the surname change issue caught my attention was via email. I had graduated from college and had started to work full-time in 2005. Around the same time, my manager sent a message with an unusual signature to our entire team. She used a double surname with one in brackets, in the form "Dilara (Kent) Stone"[1]. I never forgot that, as it meant a lot to me; it was a visual sign, a cultural code, with her feelings in between—a decision in the making. I asked her the meaning of the brackets and got the impression that she was trying to become familiar with her new identity. I felt angry and could not pin down the source of my anger; however, I suppose I knew what the brackets

---

[1] This name has been changed for privacy reasons.

meant before asking. My aim was to make her think, but of course, she had already been thinking about the issue, as the brackets indicated. At first, my question made her uncomfortable. From this visible sign, the brackets in a double-surname usage, one person can develop an opinion of another's personal life. At that point, the private inevitably becomes public.

In an interview in 1973, Austrian poet and author Ingeborg Bachmann emphasised the tension in heterosexual relationships as follows:

> [Fascism] does not start with the first bombs that are dropped; it does not start with the terror you can write about, in every newspaper. It begins in relations between people. Fascism is the primary element in the relationship between a man and a woman. (2010, viii)

Legally, women in Turkey have two options after marriage: either they have to abandon their original surname and take their husband's surname, or alternatively, they have to use both surnames. There is no option to keep their own surname, which again actually comes from another man, their father. For example, my surname journey began when I became Aydın instead of Çayır. My writing and films were published with the surname Çayır. Afterward, my legal name changed to Aydın. I did not know what to do. It was such a schizoid feeling. My identity became multiplied and I stuck with Hande Çayır Aydın in case of emergency. Some people knew my professional "Çayır" identity; legally, I had to present to people as "Aydın". It reminded me of the nonfiction bestseller (Schreiber 1973) about Sybil, the person possessed by sixteen separate identities or personalities.

Multiple personality disorder (MPD) was Sybil's "illness"[2]. She had different names and selves, plus hysteric crises. The whole identity—visually in the case of my surname, mentally in Sybil's case—breaks into pieces, and as a result, fragmented structures come into the world. Lastly, Sybil's multiple personalities are a sign of her "illness"; likewise, the changing of surnames when women marry and divorce implies a similar meaning. If a woman, for example, decides to marry sixteen times in her life, she will take on sixteen consecutive identities. With this labelling, sealing, changing surname system, the family union is protected. Thus, it is a kind of closed system that serves the patriarchy and its private properties. Furthermore, women and children end up with different surnames if a couple gets divorced.

---

[2] I used quotation marks round the word "illness" as the definition of the word changes from culture to culture, and across time periods.

Moreover, men have the right to take their surname back after a divorce, which is what happened to well-known Turkish TV personality Serap Ezgü[3]. Did this affect her financially? Has the forced surname change been a barrier for her career? How can this happen to a public figure? How does this reflect in contemporary media sources such as newspapers, advertising, television, and cinema? These questions surfaced as readily as my anger. As Goffman (1959) says in *The Presentation of Self in Everyday Life*, "When an individual appears in the presence of others, there will usually be some reason for him / [her] to mobilise his / [her] activity so that it will convey an impression to others which it is in his interests to convey" (4).

To be precise, in order to heal, I wanted to tell "my" story at first, which is referred to as "auto" in literature. Adding to that, I was curious about other women's choices, or men's thoughts on surname change issue, or even children's.[4] That part is called the "ethno", looking through "culture". While the autobiographer writes about self without other and the ethnographer studies other with as little self as possible, the autoethnographer treats self as other. Furthermore, "autoethnography calls attention to issues of power. It is about being aware of one's position in the context of research, rather than denying." (Jupp 2006, 16) Thus I, as the autoethnographer, am the instrument of data collection.

Seven years ago, my ex-husband insisted that I change my surname. I was legally Hande Aydın, *Mrs His Name*, and Mrs Private Property. Additionally, he wanted to see his surname in unofficial papers—on my business card and in my film credits. My immediate reaction was to refuse. He pushed against my refusal by insisting. Initially, it was like a joke between us. Subsequently, Sigmund Freud's *The Joke and Its Relation to the Unconscious* (2002) came into play. It was not a joke. My family was calling me "Mrs Aydın" with a smile. My second family, that is to say, my husband's family, was quite silent. In the meantime, some of my writing was published with an amoeba name: Hande

---

[3] Serap Ezgü is a well-known TV announcer who has a career of more than twenty years with the name Ezgü, and the audience know her with the surname of Ezgü. When she and her husband made the decision to divorce, the husband exercised his right to reclaim her marriage surname from her with a court decision in July of 2010. Now she is called Serap Paköz, which is a totally new name. Available at http://www.milliyet.com.tr/serap-ezgu-tarih-oldu-/gundem/sondakikagaleri/30.06.2010/1257359/default.htm (Accessed: 21 June 2019)

[4] At the very beginning I thought that this issue only applied to women, and then to men, and then children; however, as I researched, I also I came across the surname issues of LGBTIQA+ and "minorities".

Çayır Aydın. One fine day, Mrs Private Property came across a quote from Mahatma Gandhi: "You must be the change you wish to see in the world"[5]. Until that time, I did not know what to do. I was concerned about my husband whenever his friends were joking about our different surnames. We were not a symbol of a traditional family because of the non-homogeny in surname; in non-legal documents I was using my original surname, which is different from my husband's. The visual sign reflected our non-traditional relationship. He instantly gained a nickname, the "henpecked husband", just because of my surname decision. It was my name and my habituation of forming self, but remarkably families, friends, and other people felt they had the right to talk about it. Moreover, they could exact emotional power over an individual. Those people transformed into toy police in my surreal world. I thought our personal world was haunted by those toys. The end result was a decision to divorce. The reason was not only the surname change issue; it was simply the first sign of differing opinions, bitter standpoints and a rough existence. Hence, after a huge process, I became "the change I wished to see in the world".

1.2 Women's Surnames in Turkey

It seems like everyone has an opinion on what women should be able to do with their names. The author Murathan Mungan (2002) mentions in his novel *Yüksek Topuklar / High Heels* that women with two surnames are "two-faced", because on one hand they act like feminists by using two surnames, but on the other hand they reinforce the patriarchy by doing so. Mungan writes that

> for quite some time, I have had a bee in my bonnet about those women with two surnames. My God! They are many! Soon their population might equal that of the Republic of China. Add to this, whenever someone pronounces a double surname, it is always like a small victory cry [...] To me, those women who have double surnames announce that they have finally found a husband. [...] Unfortunately, it is not a random two-faced act, but rather it is a specific two-faced act that can only belong to women. [...] If you enquire, they will tell you about their difficulties in daily life, such as misfortune at a bank, unexpected things

---

[5] "The closest verifiable remark we have from Gandhi is this: 'If we could change ourselves, the tendencies in the world would also change. As a man changes his own nature, so does the attitude of the world change towards him. [...] We need not wait to see what others do.'" Available at http://www.nytimes.com/2011/08/30/opinion/falser-words-were-never-spoken.html?_r&_r=0 (Accessed: 21 June 2019)

they faced when they divorced etc., if you buy into it. (translated by me) (2002, 107)

In the end, it is a woman's surname, but almost everybody has a right to intervene except her. Hopefully, this research will represent a significant output for academia, as Turkish resources are limited to the extent that only a few major books on the subject have been published in Turkey: *Kadının Soyadı / Woman's Surname* (1999) by Nazan Moroğlu and *Kadının Soyadı ve Buna Bağlı Olarak Çocuğun Soyadı / Woman's Surname and Accordingly Surname of the Child* (2005) by Yıldız Abik. Both writers are lawyers; as a result of this, both books are written from a forensic point of view, and both lack personal stories. That is to say, it is important to produce and to share knowledge using autoethnography to tell our own stories. If not, as represented above, non-experienced individuals might speak about women's experiences, and even they write the "his-story".

There are almost no written resources on this topic. In the academic arena, the only result related to the women's changing surname issue at the national archive of the YÖK Thesis Centre is an MA thesis called *The Surname Law in Turkish Press* by Necati Gökalp, written in 1996. In addition, some feminists applied to the ECHR, which can be considered oral data and an act in its own right. Thus, there is a need to document these strong acts and vivacious motivations as a whole. The very first case from Turkey was that of Ayten Ünal Tekeli, which yielded positive results on 16 October 2004.[6] Ayten Ünal is a

---

[6] "The applicant, Ayten Ünal Tekeli, is a Turkish national, born in 1965 and living in İzmir. After her marriage on 25 December 1990 the applicant, who was then a trainee lawyer, took her husband's name pursuant to Article 153 of the Turkish Civil Code. As she was known by her maiden name in her professional life, she continued putting it in front of her legal surname. However, she could not use both names together on official documents. On 22 February 1995 the applicant brought proceedings in the Karşıyaka Court of First Instance ("the Court of First Instance") for permission to use only her maiden name, "Ünal". On 4 April 1995 the Court of First Instance dismissed the applicant's request on the ground that, under Article 153 of the Turkish Civil Code, married women had to bear their husband's name throughout their married life. An appeal by the applicant on points of law was dismissed by the Court of Cassation on 6 June 1995. The decision was served to the applicant on 23 June 1995. By one of the amendments made to Article 153 of the Civil Code on 14 May 1997, married women acquired the right to put their maiden name in front of their husband's surname. The applicant did not prefer that option because, in her view, the amendment in question did not satisfy her demand, which was to use her maiden name alone as her surname." Available at http://www.aihmiz.org.tr/?q=en/node/98 (Accessed: 21 June 2019)

feminist lawyer and her clients know her by her original surname. In the meantime, because any change in her surname could create inconvenience, she applied to the court. When Turkish Civil Law declined her case, she applied to the ECHR, and the result was positive. From that day on, she was not legally required to use the second surname.

After the Ünal Tekeli case, women in Turkey started to apply to the ECHR for their surname rights. Asuman Bayrak was one of those women who called herself a businesswoman. Focusing on Bayrak's narrative in my documentary, I saw that she made a difference in women's lives with innovative choices in the face of this imposition. When she got married in 1992, she was expected to tick a box on a form in order to use her own surname with her husband's. She failed to do it, and carried on using her original surname. However, a problem cropped up when her identity cards were stolen and she had to apply for new ones:

> When I went to apply for a new identity card, I could see that my surname was gone and had been replaced with my husband's surname. I called my lawyer about it; she said not to accept any documents. So I did not, and for two years I carried a paper that replaced my stolen ID. I did not know what to do. I got so angry. (*Yok Anasının Soyadı / Mrs His Name*: Çayır 2012)

Bayrak sought a court decision to clear up the matter, as she wanted to continue using the name that she was known by in the business world. Although the judge handling her case was a woman, the court decided against Bayrak. This goes against the commonly-held view that women will automatically stand up for the rights of other women.

> Even though the judge was a woman, she decided against me. Then we appealed to a higher court. Again the decision was against me. In any event, this process took four or five years. During that period, I lived without any identification. I could not go abroad, I could not do anything. However, eventually I had to retire. So legally we had to divorce. So we did, but we live together. In order not to change my name, we had to get divorced but we still live together. (*Yok Anasının Soyadı / Mrs His Name*: Çayır 2012)

Eventually, they appealed to the ECHR, which took several years. They finally got a decision in their favour, but the Turkish government declined to recognise the decision as valid. So if Bayrak chooses to remarry, the Turkish government will again change her surname. She is determined to fight it to the bitter end.

Thus, women face opposition in Turkey and appeal to the ECHR in order to protect their identities. Meanwhile, Ayşegül Yaraman[7], a feminist sociopolitical science professor from Turkey, emphasises the system's deadlock in this way:

> However, I do not think it is a system we could not manage. As time passes inthe marriage, a common surname or a selected one could be used. But at least, I think that today's legal system leads women into a voluntary second class, even with the law that allows the use of two surnames. (*Yok Anasının Soyadı / Mrs His Name*: Çayır 2012)

There is almost no progress on this issue in Turkey legally. Indeed, this could be solved via identity numbers; women could give their surnames to men, or an entirely new family surname for both parties could be possible. However, at this juncture, these choices are absent, leading to oppression. Keeping these women's perspectives in mind, as a counter-argument, I would like to share a man's point of view. A 49-year-old Turkish businessman and father of two, who has been married to a Western woman for more than ten years, said the following:

> My opinion is that if they did not bring it up before the marriage, then it is normal to act according to social norms. That is what I would expect. I mean, it is like saying that I do not want to do my military conscription,

---

[7] Ayşegül Yaraman, who has contributed to academia with significant books including but not limited to *Women's Political Representation in Turkey* (2000), and who uses the term "surname marriage ring" in her writing *Woman's Surname Struggle: From Partner's Surname and Hyphenated Surname to Protecting the Original Surname* (title translated by me, originally *Kadının Soyadı Mücadelesi: Eşin Soyadı ve Çift Soyadından, İlk Soyadın Korunmasına*) so as to underline the visible effects of surname pressure and to stress it as an example of "symbolic violence", which is derived from Pierre Bourdieu. It is "the violence which is exercised upon a social agent with his or her complicity. (Bourdieu and Wacquant 167) Examples of the exercise of symbolic violence include gender relations in which both men and women agree that women are weaker, less intelligent, more unreliable, and so forth (and for Bourdieu gender relations are the paradigm case of the operation of symbolic violence), or class relations in which both working-class and middle-class people agree that the middle classes are more intelligent, more capable of running the country, more deserving of higher pay."
Available at http://aysegulyaraman.com (Accessed: 21 June 2019)
Available at http://sk.sagepub.com/reference/consumerculture/n534.xml (Accessed: 21 June 2019)

but I have to. It is not an option for me. Like circumcision—everybody expects me to do it, so it is not an option, either. So this is not my option. It is not about what I want, it is bigger than that. And if the person I propose to does not say from the beginning that she wants to do something exceptional, outside the norms, I would not accept her wishes. (*Yok Anasının Soyadı* / *Mrs His Name*. Çayır 2012)

This social conditioning starts early in life. While I was in primary school, we had a classmate whose parents got divorced. One day, we went to her house for a birthday party. On the doorbell, there was an unfamiliar surname. We knew our twelve-year-old friend did not have this same surname, and we all realised that her parents were divorced. The children started to joke about it, which really hurt me. Even at that age, making light of that situation was not acceptable to me; however, while I was researching the topic, I came across similar attitudes:

Ex-husband: Okay, what is the project? Let's hear you.
Researcher / me: The project, it is called "Surname".
Ex-husband: My love, are you shooting "Surname" now?
Researcher / me: Of course!
Ex-husband: It is an unnecessary project. It is meaningless.
Researcher / me: Why?
Ex-husband: There are a lot of subjects to research.
Ex-husband: Couldn't you find anything else?
Researcher / me: Hmm, are you making light of this problem?
Ex-husband: Yes, I am making light of it.
(*Yok Anasının Soyadı* / *Mrs His Name*. Çayır 2012)

Below is another excerpt from the same conversation, including the topic of how "women get out of control" if they decide to choose their own surname and identity:

Researcher / me: Women use two surnames one after the other; it was not like that before. Why do you think it is happening now?
Ex-husband: It is like women got out of control.
Researcher / me: "Out of control", what does that mean?
Ex-husband: You do not know what "out of control" means, my love?
Researcher / me: You mean that they are in charge of their own decisions?

Ex-husband: No.

Researcher / me: Does it mean they are taking charge of...?

Ex-husband: They go wild! They go wild! So we can say they are taking charge of things. A bridle is a tool for controlling a horse. You know a bridle?

Researcher / me: Yes. Who is the horse?

Ex-husband: So it means... You control the horse by its bridle. Like you know, when you pull it, the horse stops. If the horse gets mad and out of hand when she does not obey you, the bridle is between the horse's teeth, right? She bites down hard on the bridle.

Researcher / me: Hmm...

Ex-husband: And then whatever you do, the horse does not respond, she just gets frantic. So it means, in fact, you are no longer able to control the horse. It is all gotten out of hand.

Researcher / me: So the horse is a metaphor for women, then.

Ex-husband: Yes. Do something worthwhile. Leave women's issues alone!

Researcher / me: ...

Ex-husband: Did you hear me? Did you hear me? Am I talking to the wall?

(*Yok Anasının Soyadı* / *Mrs His Name*: Çayır 2012)

Also, some men in Turkey think it is "normal" to expect a woman to take on her husband's surname:

Tea vendor: It was normal; it was not a big deal. She uses my surname. She did not ask for anything else.

Researcher / me: Did she not?

Tea vendor: No, no.

Researcher / me: And if she had?

Tea vendor: My wife does not really do that sort of thing. How can I describe it? I guess she just does not find it important.

Researcher / me: I wonder why?

Tea vendor: I do not know, I mean, I think she does not think about this stuff. She thinks about the kids and stuff like that now, she does not have energy to think about these kinds of things.

(*Yok Anasının Soyadı* / *Mrs His Name*: Çayır 2012)

Below is the story of a taxi driver who did not allow his wife to use her first surname, although his wife had graduated from university.

Taxi driver: Throughout time it has been a custom, a tradition, so it is not very logical. So to me, in the end, it is not important whether a wife uses her husband surname or not, if they are formally married on paper. So I do not know.

Researcher / me: Are you married?

Taxi driver: Yes, I am.

Researcher / me: Your wife's surname, is it yours?

Taxi driver: Yes, mine.

Researcher / me: What would you have said if she had said to you, "I am not going to use your surname, I will use mine?"

Taxi driver: Actually, my wife did say that to me.

Researcher / me: Really?

Taxi driver: My wife is a university graduate. She is a teacher. I did not allow it, I did not accept it.

(*Yok Anasının Soyadı* / *Mrs His Name*: Çayır 2012)

1.3 What Is in a Surname?

"A person's name is generally one of the first cues" (Etaugh 1999, 1) about self. The study *Names Can Never Hurt Me? The Effects of Surname Use on Perceptions of Married Women* shows that "the woman who took her husband's surname was perceived as less agentic than women who kept their maiden name or hyphenated their name" (Etaugh 1999, 1). On the other hand, the article "Sharing Surnames: Children, Family, Kinship" by Hayley Davies presents children's perspectives on surnames and shows that surnames are meaningful to children, assist the cultural family imagery, and strengthen kinship relations. In Davies' (2011) field notes, we witness the story of Hannah, who has been known in school as Hannah Sheilder-Scott. She stresses that she does not want to be called Sheilder, because that is her father's name; she hates him and he is not in her life anymore. In other words, the use of surnames is the visual sign that kinship is constituted or denied.

Among other things, can taking on a man's surname after marriage be empowering? As one could always be certain of who the mother of a child was, it might serve another objective. To that point, we can examine a study called *What's in a Name? The Significance of the Choice of Surnames Given to Children Born within Lesbian-Parent Families* by Kathryn Almack (2005), as it focuses on family practices and boundaries. Biological mothers' roles in naming "sperm bank" babies challenge the structure of heterosexual family decisions, and the question arises: are homosexual family structures possible with their own parameters, or are those the only copies of the current system? Homosexual sex does not involve procreation, but desire; because there are two penises or two vaginas, making a baby is impossible, as is also mentioned in Lee Edelman's work *No Future: Queer Theory and Death Drive.* Consequently (2004), in this system, there is no future, no generation, and no surnames at all.

The heterosexual family institution is also questioned by Talat Parman's article "Merhaba Bebek Merhaba Aile: Bireyin Doğumu ve Adlandırma" / "Hello Baby Hello Family: The Birth of the Individual and Giving a Name":

> The very first method to humiliate people, even make them non-human, starts with namelessness. If you erase people's names, then you make them invisible. Even in the Nazi concentration camps, it is the absolute reason that people have no names but numbers on bracelets. (2007, 43-56) (translated by me)

1.4 The Duality of Women and Men

The appearance of polarities or dualities can be understood in the absence of one half or the other, such as with subject/object, nature/culture, East/West, heart/brain, art/science, femininity/masculinity, myth-experience/knowledge, private/public, subjective/objective, and individual/society. In other words, meaning is generated by opposition, by an analytic category from Structuralism, which is a principal of Saussurian linguistics. The terms are mutually exclusive. On the other hand, ambiguities are produced by this logic. For instance, in between "me"/"us" and "them" there are deviants, dissidents. In anthropology, the ambiguous boundary between two acknowledged categories is where taboo appears. In terms of the whole, these deviants, "maybe-persons" instead of "yes-no-persons" might be communicable in a given regime of truth.

According to Western metaphysics (Curthoys 2003, 110; Klages 2006, 54) one of the binary oppositions, for example, West, is right, powerful, and dominant, and "the other", for example, East, is lacking. Historically and conceptually, comprehending the hermeneutic approach[8] and the post-modern orientation of it[9] is important when it comes to binary hierarchies. Hence, binary opposition is highly productive of ideological meanings. As Michel Foucault (1980) says, "each society has its regime of truth, its general politics of truth that is the types of discourse which it accepts and makes function as true; the mechanisms and instances which enable one to distinguish true and false statements, the means by which each is sanctioned the techniques and procedures accorded value in

---

[8] i.e. Heidegger and Gadamer.
[9] i.e. Derrida and Lyotard.

the acquisition of truth, the status of those who are charged with saying what counts as true". (131) Furthermore, does this system exist because West/culture/brain/men exclude East/nature/heart/women, or is there any continuation between them from which to cleave or evolve?

In Asma Barlas' work *Believing Women in İslam: Unreading Patriarchal Interpretations of the Qur'an* (2009), the duality of women and men is represented thus:

> Indeed, if İslam were to designate women and men as opposites (man as the "self" and women as the "other", man as having and woman as lacking something), it could not reasonably hold them to identical standards of moral praxis; lacking knowledge, rationality, the ability to reason (attributes associated with the masculine/self), women would be unable to understand, or act upon, Divine Truth. The Qur'an does not define women and men in terms of sex or gender attributes; rather, it teaches that humans were created self (nafs) possess the same attributes, and have the same capacity for moral choice, reasoning, and individuality. (103)

1.5 Answering a Bank's Question: What Is Your Mother's "Maiden" Name?[10]

In a world where women are so-called "lacking" it can be possible to erase their stories by erasing their surnames. Corporate institutions such as banks ask for one's "mother's maiden name" as a password in order to protect crucial ID information. The perception is that it is safe, a secret, and not known anymore; it has been forgotten, erased from history. Gilmore (1994) notes that one's mother's "maiden" name is perceived as something that only the individual would know, whereas the patronym represents both public identity and authority:

> The "name of the father" and the mother's maiden name represent different orders of knowledge and explain the cultural ambivalence many women feel about our names. Such binary distinctions are definitional strategies, part of the production and maintenance of the technologies of truth and linked to their hierarchising organisations of knowledge—here, the gendered distinction between secret and legal

---

[10] I chose "surname" rather than "last name" or "family name", and although there is a connection with the term "chastity belt", I used "maiden name" rather than "birth name" or "pre-marriage" name because of its ubiquity in the vernacular. I recognise that this usage is problematic. This footnote is inspired by Wilson. (2009, 9)

(private and public). This play on authority, staged through the recording of the mother's maiden name as "secret" in order to enforce the "public" authority of the name of the father, reveals a structuring antithesis in names (88).

A woman's name and surname is the ID by "which she is known" and "her achievements are associated" (Lamber 1973, 779) with this ID in the long run. We as women expect our laws are reasonable; however, the global case of banks using a mother's "maiden" name as a secret password underlines another issue which is not only dealing with the law but also cultural values, tradition, and society's soul. Even if equal-opportunity legislation passes, studies show that women will maintain their traditional position within the family. Moreover, how about those who have no mothers at all? Whose surname will they use as a password? These issues surround the question of the true function of a surname.

Chapter 2

Methodology

2.1 What Is Autoethnography?

Simply put, auto means self, narrator, I; ethno means others, communities, cultures, they, we, society, nation, state; graphy means writing, and the process. In other words, autoethnography is a qualitative research method (Ngunjiri, Hernandez, and Chang 2010) that focuses on self-study, where researchers are using data from their personal life stories as a means to understand society. While I was digging deeper into autoethnography, although the definition was quite simple and transparent, I bumped up against another frustrating question from a scholar: "Isn't it too subjective, and too confusing? What is the difference between an autoethnographic thesis and a novel?"[1] In their article "Autoethnography is a Queer Method", Stacy Holman Jones and Tony E. Adams (2010) collected some of the more provocative "too" examples mentioned above:

> Autoethnography and queer theory are both also often criticised for being too much and too little—too much personal mess, too much theoretical jargon, too elitist, too sentimental, too removed, too difficult, too easy, too white, too Western, too colonialist, too indigenous. Yet at the same time, too little artistry, too little theorising, too little connection between the personal and political, too impractical, too little fieldwork, too few real-world applications. (e.g. Alexander 2003, Anderson 2006, Atkinson 1997, Atkinson and Delamont 2006, Barnard 2004, Buzard 2003, Gans 1999, Gingrich-Philbrook 2005, Halberstam 2005, Johnson 2001, Kong, Mahoney and Plummer 2002, Lee 2003,

---

[1] *The Ethnographic I: A Methodological Novel about Autoethnography,* by Carolyn Ellis, gives an answer to all of these dilemmas. First of all, the book's name itself implies that it can be a methodology and novel at the same time. "Expressing concrete lived experience via narrative modes" (Ellis and Bochner 1996) emphasises experimental forms of qualitative writing in academia with such subtitles as *"Autoethnography in Interview Research", "Putting the Self into Research", "Issues of Memory and Truth",* and *"Thinking Like an Ethnographer, Writing Like a Novelist".*

Madison 2006, Owen 2003, Perez 2005, Watson 2005, Yep and Elia 2007)
(Nash and Kath 195)

As an academically-recognized methodology[2], autoethnography follows a
social scientific inquiry, and has been expected to be analysed in a broad sense
of socio-cultural context. Conjointly, "connecting the personal to the cultural"
is also affirmed in writing of pioneers Ellis and Bochner. (2000, 739) To put it in
another way, in grounded everyday life autoethnography explicitly works
against traditional approaches and conventional academic critics and
disciplines. By doing so, marginal experiences—usually the invisible ones—are
represented while focusing on fluidity, subjectivity, responsiveness,
transformation, and contribution. Researchers understand and analyse
themselves as well as society by the help of autoethnography, which is also a
researcher- and reader-friendly method. Thus, sharing the output leads to
transformation and to the development of cultural sensitivity. Madden (2010)
makes a point on this transformation:

> Despite the strict meaning of the term, reflexivity is not really about
> "you, the ethnographer"; it is still about "them, the participants". The
> point of getting to know "you, the ethnographer" better, getting to know
> the way you influence your research, is to create a more reliable portrait,
> argument or theory about "them, the participants". (23)

As the passage above indicates subjectivity, it is therefore not a problem from
Madden's point of view. Correspondingly, Carolyn Ellis stresses autoethnography's
goal in *The Ethnographic I: A Methodological Novel About Autoethnography*
(2004) that she as an academic starts her work with her personal life and pays
attention to her physical feelings, thoughts, and emotions. Ellis uses
"emotional recall"[3] and "systematic sociological introspection" (1991, 32) to try
to understand an experience she has lived through. The goal is to penetrate into

---

[2] Autoethnographic output is being published in numerous academic contexts, including
but not limited to *Qualitative Inquiry*, the *Journal of Advanced Nursing*, the *Journal of
Contemporary Ethnography*, the *Journal of Sociology*, the *Journal of Career Development*,
Cultural Studies, the *Journal of Transformative Education*, *The Journal of Men's Studies*,
and Public Relations Inquiry. In addition, 1361 pages are listed while searching for
autoethnographic articles on the Sage Journals homepage, and each page includes 10
articles, which means there are 13,610 published articles on Sage alone in 2016.

[3] In her book *The Ethnographic I: A Methodological Novel about Autoethnography*, Ellis
uses a chapter subtitle called "Taking Autoethnographic Fieldnotes, Capturing
Experience, Memory and Emotional Recall", and stresses emotions and their value.

the concrete details of life, and understand oneself in deeper ways. According to Ellis (2004), "autoethnography means research, writing story, and process that bridge the autobiographical, personal to cultural, social and political". Principally, the leading way to engage in how to do autoethnography is to go out and do it. "Writing vulnerably, evocatively and ethically" (2004, 119) is the core element of this method. Instead of dealing with hypotheses, the emphasis would be a process of slice-of-life discovery. Because a thesis takes a long time and demands a lot of energy, the research should be done by a researcher who is deeply engaged in it. To see the matter in a new light, not only the researcher's work but also his/her personal life is critiqued in autoethnography. As such, the response from others can often be painful and they will possibly make certain judgements. Ultimately, it can be said that researchers do not choose autoethnography, yet the method itself chooses its lucky victims.

In autoethnography, researchers give voice to stories that assist in improving readers', authors', and participants' lives, and the output highlights emotional experience. According to Spence, "rather than believing in the presence of an external, unconstructed truth, researchers on this end of the continuum embrace narrative truth, which means that the experiences they depict become believable, lifelike, and possible" (1982, 43-69). Stories in autoethnography stimulate others to tell theirs. Also, to write about self means documenting social experience, and displaying layers of consciousness. Similarly, Sexton Finck (2009) emphasises why she embarked in her autoethnographic project; it is because she wanted to understand this desire, subjectivity, and agency as a filmmaker and researcher more comprehensively (11). She continues by stressing her own perspective, her own subjectivity, and her own agency which is not fixed, but is an ongoing process. Rather than assuming they do not exist, Ruth Behar (2014) emphasises our thinking is not separated from our feelings. Boylorn, Robin M., and Mark P. Orbe (2013) on the other hand, emphasise our everyday lives as follows:

> Autoethnography is oftentimes serendipitous, occurring when we are going about our everyday lives. Autoethnography is also therapeutic, embodied (Berry 2012), performative (Spry 2001), and queer (Adams and Holman Jones 2008), speaking from, for, and to the margins. (18)

According to Marxists, the self is a product of the ideology of historical periods. To psychoanalysts, it is determined unconsciously. On one hand, some French thinkers such as Barthes (2001) have placed significance on self. To Foucault (1988) knowledge is integral to power and subjectivity relations. On the other hand, feminists and post-colonialists are critical of the reduction of the human subject, self. In short, the tension between individual agency and cultural constitution has been perpetually discussed in many disciplines. To sum up, "the individual 'I' does not exist alone, but with another, which is to say being one is never singular, but always implies and indeed embodies another" (Lebow 2012, 2-3). So, "the 'I' is always social, always ready in relation" (3) and when researcher singular "I" speaks, ontologically, it is in effect, the researcher plural "we", and it can even be understood to be a "research of us" rather than a "research of me".[4]

To put it another way, in this case as a methodology, even on its meaning in the name, "auto [self] ethno [culture] graphy" can be considered as a way of transcending duality conflicts, as the "self" and "external self" are together, "but the stages are not mutually exclusive" (Ellis 2004, 119). In the opposition of "self" and "the other", these refer to and create each other; one becomes true with the existence of the other.

2.2 History of Autoethnography

Researchers' experience was not viewed as legitimate until works in anthropology challenged the boundaries of self-studying in the seventies and early eighties (Taylor 2000, 58-73). The term autoethnography was first coined in 1975 by the anthropologist Heider (3-17). Since then, according to Ellis and Bochner's (2000) research, a variety of labels have been used to refer the term, such as

> autobiographical ethnography, auto-biology, auto-observation, auto-pathography, collaborative autobiography, complete-member research, confessional tales, critical autobiography, emotionalism narratives of the self, ethno-biography, ethnographic autobiography, ethnographic memoir, ethnographic poetics, ethnographic short stories, evocative narratives, experiential texts, first-person accounts, indigenous ethnography, interpretive biography, literary tales, lived experience, narrative ethnography, native ethnography, new or experimental ethnography, opportunistic research, personal essays, personal ethnography, personal experience narrative, personal narratives, personal writing, postmodern

---

[4] Alisa Lebow says that "Despite the fact that we believe it to express our individuality, it nonetheless also expresses our commonality, our plurality, our interrelatedness with a group, a mass, a sociality, if not a society. This is as true about the expression of individuality and subjectivity in first-person films as it is in language itself. And that is precisely what the opposite, in most cases, of the singular 'I', and can even be understood to be a 'cinema of we', rather than a 'cinema of me.'" (2012, 3)

ethnography, radical empiricism, reflexive ethnography, self-ethnography, self-stories, socio-autobiography, socio-poetics, and writing-stories. (733-768)

Additionally, postmodern, poststructuralist, feminist researchers were clashing on issues of authority, voice, and method. For example, Geertz (1973), Clifford and Marcus (1986), and Marcus and Fischer (1999) "prepared a space for new forms of expressing lived experience" and "deconstructed writing conventions" (Ellis 2004, 17). Viewing "the personal is political", autoethnographic work engages how we think about knowledge. Furthermore, in the 1980s, new forms of social science inquiry appeared, inspired by postmodernism, where scholars understood new relationships between writers, readers, and texts. For instance, Roland Barthes and Jacques Derrida realised that stories were constitutive and complex. Derrida (1987) argues this representation of any content in writing and even offers silence and gaps.

As a matter of fact, scholars of self-narratives consider St. Augustine's Confessions from the 4th century. Up until now, for example, Indian political activist Mahatma Gandhi and civil rights activist Rosa Parks (1997), as many others, added "formality to the genre of self-narratives" (Chang 2008, 36). In addition, an excerpt from Maya Angelou's (1997) autobiography *I Know Why the Caged Bird Sings* represents momentous, self-affirmative writing. In order to resist orthodox methods or sterile approaches, these scholars started to consider literature rather than physics. Conventional ways of conducting research were limiting race, gender, sexuality, age, ability, and class-oriented topics, and mostly "advocating a white, masculine, heterosexual, upper-classed, able-bodied perspective" (Ellis and Bochner 2011, 273-290). In this respect, autoethnography opens up a new window and lessens these rigid definitions. Accordingly, autoethnographic scholars give voice to silenced and marginalised experiences and "do not distinguish doing research from living life" (Boylorn, Robin M., and Mark P. Orbe 2013, 15) throughout history; however, this did not have a name until relatively recently.

2.3 Research Topics in Autoethnography

In terms of autoethnographic enquiries, sexual abuse, illness, motherhood, father-son relationships, Jewish identity, Black identity, getting a PhD, and many other subjects, that is to say, all aspects of life, can be studied. To illustrate, working with a patient might limit research due to privacy issues; in that case, the autoethnographer seeks advice from his/her personal experience so as to interpret the data in an advantageous way. Chang (2008) argues that "autoethnography should be ethnographic in its methodological orientation, cultural in its interpretive orientation, and autobiographical in its content orientation" (48). As opposed to ethnographers, autoethnographers enter the research field with a familiar topic, self, whereas ethnographers begin their research with others. Even more, Ellis's approach to these familiar topics is usually "heartfelt" and "evocative". *The Power of Feelings* (1999) creates personal meaning in potential topics that are linked to cultural construction (Chodorow 164).

Some researchers select a more specific topic such as Korean female identity, or some topics may be more personal; there is no limit. For example, Tompkins' *A Life in School* (1996) has an autoethnographic quality although Tompkins has not explicitly labelled the work (Chang 2008, 50). Finally, the publisher of the Left Coast Press, Mitch Allen, who has 35 years of experience in academic publishing and also holds a PhD in archaeology, notes that whatever the topic:

> An autoethnographer must look at experience analytically. Otherwise [you are] telling [your] story—and that is nice—but people do that on Oprah [a US-based television programme] every day. Why is your story more valid than anyone else's? What makes your story more valid is that you are a researcher. You have a set of theoretical and methodological tools and a research literature to use. That's your advantage. If you cannot frame it around these tools and literature and just frame it as "my story," then why or how should I privilege your story over anyone else's I see 25 times a day on TV? (Personal interview, May 4, 2006) (Ellis, Adams, Bochner 2011, 273)

2.4 Data Collection in Autoethnography

The question of "why" assists researchers in planning their needs and defining the purpose of the research, and perfectly helps the data collection: why does someone want to study him/herself? How will someone collect the data about the self? How will s/he manage the interpretation process? What will be the outcomes? (Chang 2008, 61) First, the researcher's issues, concerns and memories create the initial phase. "Something significant happened to me" and "I am curious about others' experience on a specific issue" are possible starting points. Those questions in my mind gave me the opportunity to research more via data collection, and assisted me in finding my path.

Although one's life experience sheds light to shape the data, a literature review is also highly recommended in the process as described by Chang (2008, 35). By doing so, according to Chang, the researcher carries personal and cultural baggage. The researcher's identity is vital to opportunities, insights and innovations. Personal interest makes the research passionate, and this significance indicates professional development. Undoubtedly, strangers can be connected to self through many group members, while authors are the main narrators. Ethnographic data is based on words but usually there are no numbers coming from field notes, journals or interviews during the research process (Chang 2008, 89). Also, Van Maanen remarks on the relationship between the observed, the observer, the tale, and the audience:

> [...] a discussion of ethnographic writing needs to consider a few elements in order to understand the way the story comes across. [...] (1) the assumed relationship between culture and behaviour, the observed; (2) the experiences of the fieldworker, the observer; (3) the representational style selected to join the observer and observed, the tale; (4) the role of the reader engaged in the active reconstruction of the tale, the audience. This means we need to look at research, reflection, writing and reading in an overall understanding of ethnography. (2011, xi)

In addition to textual data, audio recordings, moving graphics, and even cultural songs might be collected, involving keen observations of complex human experiences. Memory certainly distorts the past, though some memories are vivid. While collecting data, fragments of the past contributed by the researcher, namely, an autobiographical timeline will help. Thematically focusing on this timeline will allow the researcher to zoom in on thinking, perceiving, and evaluating the process. Chronological, annual, seasonal, weekly, and daily listing of major events leads to significant personal and cultural discovery.

In the free writing process, I witnessed that proverbs help unexpectedly. According to Chang (2008), listing to repeated names in the family or in an extended community or society impacts the researcher's life as well as the research, and the researcher gains a broad understanding of thought, belief, and behaviour. Furthermore, in Chang's view, related rituals and celebrations are significant tools to consider. Mentors have a significant impact on individuals, and inevitably affect the narration. Visualising kinship diagrams might create self. Free drawings are another visual strategy to collect autoethnographic data.

In this intimate methodology, self-observation is a must: "what you say", "what you think", "which objects you remember most", and "whom you include or exclude". That is to say, to get in tune with the self is keenly important: "how are you feeling" and "how are you interpreting the situation". Simultaneously, the researcher has to step outside of the possible event as a primary element. Subsequently, a good writer is willing to be vulnerable; in other words, the researcher as a research tool is able to see him/herself in a vulnerable position in the core of the autoethnography.

2.5 Researcher as Researched Subject

As an emerging researcher I value collaboration, with multiple—mostly marginal and silenced—voices as an activist inquiry while creating meaning, suffering, and observing at a deeper level, a reconstructive approach in the challenging ways of reasoning about truth, and sharing. From the eye of first-person—me—photographs, video artworks, and even scribbling are useful in the process, as well as social maps, school records, and interviews of those who had a similar experience. I recorded my interactions with total strangers, opponents whom I did not like, and acquaintances whom I did not know well. Subjective feelings and objective facts were collected as well, from visual arts to psychology, and cinema to cultural studies.

Chang (2008) refers to four types of autoethnography: descriptive-realistic writing, confessional-emotive writing, analytical-interpretive writing, and imaginative-creative writing (84). My preferences lean predominantly toward the last one, imaginative-creative writing, and also confessional-emotive, which overlaps with Carolyn Ellis' (2004) work (9). In understanding qualitative research, these autoethnographers explain how autoethnographic research enables us to live better and argue that stories allow us to lead more reflective, meaningful lives. Although the methodology itself might have been criticised as being narcissistic, Chang (2008) mentions "a therapeutic effect" (51) on authors and readers.

Initially, realistic-descriptive narratives focus on places, people, and experiences as accurately as possible with detailed descriptions. For example, *Memories of the Soul* by Phifer (2011) realistically triggers the reader's attention. In this style, the writing represents a story. Also, pioneers of autoethnography, for example Spry, Ellis, and Adams, usually encourage writers to add many details as possible. Writers even remove themselves at the beginning from the picture that they describe. In autoethnography though, it is not possible to remove one's own self totally. Secondly, in confessional-emotive writing the researcher is free to express confusion and dilemmas in life (Chang 2008, 145). *My Mother Is Mentally Retarded* by Ronai (1996) is a progressive and a regressive narrative, and carries a painful experience which can be evaluated as a good example of confessional-emotional writing (109). On one hand, autoethnographers' vulnerable self-exposure evokes empathy, and on the other hand, this version is sometimes marked as an "emotional catharsis" (Spence 1982, 43-69). The third subtitle is called analytical-interpretive writing, and *Beyond the Whiteness of Whiteness: Memoir of a White Mother of Black Sons* by Jane Lazarre (1996) can be considered an example in which the author not only analyses the impact of race in her own life, but also interprets the issue of race in a broader context. Imaginative-creative writing form, finally, is 180 degrees removed from conventional academic style. Various genres such as drama, documentary, and even poetry have been used. Experimental autoethnography opens up possible creative solutions: *A Secret Life in a Culture of Thinness* (Tillmann 1996, 76).

Furthermore, in *Becoming a Reflexive Researcher: Using Our Selves in Research*, Kim Etherington (2004) discussed the process of how to do research:

> Academic research has traditionally been seen as an impersonal activity: researchers have been expected to approach their studies objectively, and we were taught that rigour demanded they adopt a stance of distance and non-involvement and subjectivity was a contaminant. This "God's eye view" of the world can seem unchallengeable, expert, hard to connect with, and sometimes for me, uninteresting to read. (25)

The research-informed short film *Rufus Stone* (2012), a three-year funded research project led by Kip Jones, is a good example of this non-"God's eye view" approach. Patricia Levy (2012), in her article called "A Review of Rufus Stone: The Promise of Arts-Based Research" describes the film in the following way:

> The film tells the story of a young man in rural England who, while developing an attraction to another young man, is viciously outed by small-minded village people. He flees to London and returns home 50 years later and is forced confront the people from his past and larger issues of identity and time. This essay considers *Rufus Stone* as both a film and as a work of arts-based research. I suggest *Rufus Stone* is not only a terrific film but it also represents the best of arts-based research and public scholarship more broadly. (1)

After watching *Rufus Stone*, following the academic work of these autoethnographers, exploring examples of arts-based research, and "connecting with a wide variety of audiences"[5], including those in teaching, community groups, and support organisations for LGBTIQA+ and the ageing, I turned my focus toward my story. Depending on the purpose, mixed styles may also be used and combined with one another. As an educated, feminist, divorced woman from Turkey, my individual culture is intentionally composed of all forms of art, and cross-sections of social norms. As Chang (2008) discusses, "every piece of writing reflects the disposition of its author. This book is not an exception; it subtly and explicitly reveals who I am and what I value" (10). Thus, this research represents my professional interest in self-narratives, identity politics, human rights, and representation of female subjectivity. As far as I studied in my BA degree, Visual Arts and Visual Communication Design, and in my MA degree, Cinema and Television, most of the time I used autoethnographic methods in order to express my thoughts and feelings in my projects, without knowing that particular term. Finally, I found a book called *Method Meets Art: Art-Based Research Practice* (2015) by Patricia Levy, which was another indication that I was walking the right path.

If traditional methods cannot capture these innovative approaches, then narrative inquiry, music, performance, poetry, dance, and visual art represent new ways to research. After looking through the culture and framing with theories, it is a reasonable assumption that the output will also be short stories, photographic personal essays, and fragmented writing. Consequently, this research has the potential to be confessional, emotional, therapeutic, creative, and unconventional in order to reconstruct academic knowledge.

---

[5] Available at https://blogs.bournemouth.ac.uk/research/2014/10/19/rufus-stone-goes-live-and-free-on-the-internet/ (Accessed: 21 June 2019)

Chapter 3

Theory

3.1 Equality Now: Am I a Feminist?

In our daily lives, in academia, and in almost all our possible surroundings around us, we come across numerous labels that might have wider connotations: he is a terrorist; she is an anti-militarist; he is a fascist; she is a feminist. Moreover, what one person understands from the word "feminist" might be different from another person's view. When I say "I am a feminist" about myself, in this specific case, my understanding of feminism needs to be discussed, as labels shape our perceptions and change our minds. Correspondingly, am I feminist? Before all else, I admit I do not believe strictly in yes/no questions and answers, but rather a detailed expression. At the end of this chapter, the judgement will be yours.

I have been interested in given-gender roles since I was ten, when my father started asking me to bring him tea. On the other hand, my brother, who is only three years older than I am, did not serve anything. From that day on, I questioned why my mother and I serve the men at home while they literally never did this job for us, or even for themselves. At the age of twelve, when I was playing with my friends in the street, I was instructed to be home before dark. My brother however was again privileged: he came home whenever he wanted to. At the age of fifteen, I was asked to wear t-shirts that covered the top halves of my arms; conversely, my brother experienced a totally different world, that is to say, man's world, and there were almost no restrictions for him. Furthermore, when I was trying to go abroad at the age of eighteen, there were assumptive questions regarding whether I was planning on being a prostitute. Years later, when I was getting married, my father advised me that if I were to divorce, he would take the honour-killing attitude that I could not come back to the family home again, even though I had already lived on my own for nine years. In his head, it was certainly a joke; however, he suddenly forgot his funny jokes when my brother was getting married. In short, a lot of experiences have occurred in my family life that helped me to see that I was different from my brother just because of my gender. The reflection of my reaction to the surname change issue is not a specific case for naming perplexity, but an entire identity boycott.

This is not only about me; women throughout Turkey's history have resisted these identity issues. For example, on the topic of surnames, I came across an author, Cahit Uçuk (1911-2014), who never changed her surname even after four marriages. She admired and followed the work of Halide Edip, and reacted to the surname situation:

> [Uçuk] likes Halide Edip most. [...] However, Edip's signature changed after a marriage, and she signed as Halide Salih. One year later, she would be Halide Edip Adıvar. [...] She thought that since Halide Edip was a well-known author and she thought that there was no need for this surname change at all. (translated by me)[1]

As first-wave feminism focused on women's voting rights, that is to say, legal rights and issues of equality, Cahit Uçuk's demand is an understandable one. Fatma Aliye (1862-1936), for example, acquired the surname "Topuz" after the surname law came into effect. According to Yaraman's (1992) book *Elinin Hamuruyla Özgürlük / Freedom with Dough of Your Hand*[2] in 1890 Fatma Aliye also signed her translation book *Meram* (Volonté by Georges Ohnet), with the name "A Woman" (67). Behice Boran (1910-1987), an active politician, author and sociologist, was known for being fired from the Academy because of her views and was the first Turkish woman socialist member of Parliament who never deviated from her first surname after marriage. According to an anecdote, the head of a meeting called her "Hatice 'T'atko Boran" instead of Behice Boran, where 'H'atko[3] was her husband's surname; the subsequent fallout was so intense that the person in question was disciplined by a superior. Boran was adamant about never using her husband's surname.

Another instance of a surname issue from this period is that of Şükûfe Nihal (1896-1973), who wrote an article for a newspaper at the age of thirteen regarding women's education rights, at a time when women were rarely seen in newspapers. Although she married twice, she never used anything other than her first surname, and preferred to be called either Nihal or Şükûfe Nihal[4]. Furthermore, Füruzan (born 1932) never used a surname as an author. The

---

[1] Available at https://www.hurriyet.com.tr/gundem/koca-soyadi-alan-halide-edipe-inat-cahit-ucuk-oldu-122589 (Accessed: 11 June 2019)
[2] The book is signed as Ayşegül Yaraman-Başbuğu, and at the time it was asserted that this was the first double surname usage on a book cover in Turkey.
[3] Available at http://www.amargidergi.com/yeni/?p=1880 (Accessed: 11 June 2019)
[4] Available at http://www.amargidergi.com/yeni/?p=2060#more-2060 (Accessed: 10 June 2019)

actress Melek Kobra[5] (1915-1939), on the other hand, used four different surnames even though she only lived to the age of 24. Initially, she used "Sabahattin", her father's surname. After the Surname Law went into effect, the family took on the surname "Ezgi". She then married Ferdi Tayfur and became Melek Tayfur. When her journal was discovered after her death, however, she had signed all the entries "Melek Kobra", a name that she had chosen.

As an author, Nezihe Muhiddin[6] (1889-1958) preferred not to use her husband's surname during her literary career; Muhiddin is her father's surname. Likewise, anchorwoman and journalist Jülide Gülizar (1929-2011) did not use her father's surname "Göksan", instead creating the surname "Gülizar" to sign her work. As she says with her own words in Özlem Bayraktar's work *Ekranda Bir Kadın Olarak Kendine Yer Açmak / Making a Room for Yourself as a Woman on the Screen* (2016), "a lot of women artists change their surname when they get married. When they divorce, it changes again. This reduces their reputation to zero when they announce their new name" (152). When she became popular, people maliciously called her father by her surname, which made her father quite angry. Her father's reply is meaningful in this respect: "Dear wife, tell your daughter Jülide that she does not use my surname; but do not give her surname to me" (153).

Author Sevgi Soysal (1936-1976) also used different surnames in her career, such as "Nutku" for her first book *Tutkulu Perçem* in 1962 and "Sabuncu" for her second book *Tante Rosa* in 1968. Aysegül Yaraman emphasised (2015) the following in the article "Sorunları mı Sorumluluktan, Sorumluluğu mu Sorunlarından: Kadınlık Durumu, Kadınlık Bilinci ve Sevgi Soysal" / "Problems Caused by Responsibility or Responsibility Caused by Their Problems: Femininity Condition, Femininity Consciousness and Sevgi Soysal":

> Sevgi Soysal never used the surname she was born with. She acquired three different surnames from different men and published her work under these different surnames. Both her life and work document the specific period of time in which there are contradictions where the woman is both the witness and the accused. There are traces of women's struggles that have happened before. [...] In her short life, Sevgi Soysal used four different surnames, and this legal situation mirrors the struggle of the '80s in which women sought to use their father's and

---

[5] Available at https://www.haberler.com/melek-kobra-nin-bilinmeyen-hikayesi-5161215-haberi/ (Accessed: 10 June 2019)

[6] Available at http://www.lacivertdergi.com/portre/ornek-kadinlar/2014/12/30/kadin-haklarina-adanmis-bir-omur-nezihe-muhiddin (Accessed: 11 June 2019)

husband's surnames together. They later got that right, and in 2000, women struggle to have the option not to change their surname at all. (translated by me) (35-49)

A surname is a label that implies who the father is. We all know from the pregnant woman's visible body that baby is inside; however, we have no clue about the father, and the surname highlights the father's existence. Whether advantageous or not, the paternal surname tradition became the target of activists in the *Soyadına Sahip Çık / Claim Your Surname Campaign*[7] in 2009. The involved names included but were not limited to a former member of the Grand National Assembly of Turkey Işılay Saygın, the Turkish Mothers Organisation, students, housewives, lawyers, and doctors. As women have to change all their ID documents such as their passport and driving license after a marriage or divorce, it brings not only a practical burden but also an economic one. Each time they change their surnames they have to pay, so much so that on 20 February 2010, an extraordinary incident occurred in which Fadime Şanlı[8] was killed by her husband, and because she did not write in Facebook that she was married and using her birth surname, the judge reduced the sentence from life imprisonment to 16 years, according to journalist Ezgi Başaran's article on 18 February 2015 in the *Radikal* newspaper.

Singer Müşerref Akay was also initially known by the surname "Tezcan"; however, when she divorced, she was forced to give up the surname, because her ex-husband did not want her to keep it. Although the system and some husbands insist on giving a new surname to a woman when she gets married, they take it back when the agreement goes downhill. I even personally know a clerk who conspired to protect surname unions, and deliberately did their job as slowly as possible.

Turkish Airlines[9] is another example of pressure to unite family names, with a campaign in which partners travelling under the same surname receive a discount of 20%. Furthermore, some of my female friends have very long surnames or masculine ones that they would like to change; however, I have also seen double-barrelled surnames like Hanzade Doğan Boyner or Ümit Boyner Sabancı, where the Doğan, Boyner and Sabancı families' surnames

---

[7] Available at http://www.ntv.com.tr/yasam/bosanan-kadinlar-icin-soyadinasahipcik-com, O2q62mZ7OUuaE44oo7wzRQ (Accessed: 3 June 2019)

[8] Available at http://www.radikal.com.tr/yazarlar/ezgi-basaran/feministim-size-emaneti-gosteriyorum-1295587/ (Accessed: 2 June 2019)

[9] Available at https://www.sabah.com.tr/ekonomi/2015/11/12/thy-yuzde-20-soyadi-indirimi-yapiyor (Accessed: 3 June 2019)

represent not only a personal decision, but also a combination of very famous families, statures, and brands. What is the function of a surname, then?

The same logic applies when it comes to foreign surnames. For example, Turkish media personality Hande Ataizi married Benjamin Harvey, a foreign national, and became Hande Harvey. As "Harvey" is an international surname, newspapers wrote that it was very attractive: she is so lofty![10] On the other hand, in popular media we saw a famous woman singer, Seda Sayan, who had relationships and marriages with younger men, which threatened the hegemonic system. She never changed her surname. Bestselling author Elif Şafak prefers to use her mother's name as a surname. Lawyer and sociologist Nermin Abadan Unat[11] is known by two surnames. At the age of 93, Professor Abadan Unat brought the issue of double surnames to the court, asserting that it was problematic to pass through airports in order to attend conventions, meetings or symposiums. "Abadan" is her surname, which was acquired from her late first husband. In her court filing, she noted the following:

> Invitations from abroad create a distressing problem, in that "Nermin Unat" and "Nermin Abadan Unat" are the same person, but I cannot prove it. To solve at least this issue, I would like to use my two husbands' surnames together.[12] (translated by me)

Moreover, lawyer-activist Hülya Gülbahar has allowed me to share the following excerpt from an email in the Purple Roof Women's Shelter Foundation's online group:

> *Dear Friends,*
> *I had no time to write before.*
> *My case regarding the surname issue has been accepted in a local court.*
> *However, the Civil Registry opposed it.*
> *As for the Supreme Court of Appeals?*
> *They support husbands and want them to be in the case.*
> *It is a disaster.*

---

[10] Available at http://www.hurriyet.com.tr/hande-harvey-cok-havali-oldu-23204154 (Accessed: 5 June 2019)

[11] Available at http://www.cumhuriyet.com.tr/haber/turkiye/56575/iki_kocasinin_da_ soyadini _istedi.html (Accessed: 20 June 2019)

[12] Available at http://www.cumhuriyet.com.tr/haber/turkiye/56575/iki_kocasinin_da_ soyadini _istedi.html (Accessed: 21 March 2020)

If the husband declines, then what?
In short, we have the ECHR decisions in our favour, but the Supreme
Court of Appeals still would like to see the husband's view.
In other words, it is a lie when the media says the surname issue is solved.
It is not solved.
It is dangerous.
We went through the entire struggle.
This means we have to start from the beginning again after our entire
struggle.
We do not accept this.
I have just sent a rectification to Supreme Court of Appeals.
Let's keep an eye on that.[13] (translated by me)

I remember Duygu Asena's words in *Orada Kadınlar Var Mı / Are There Women There*, compiled by Şadan Maraş Öymen as follows:

> I saw an invitation card with "Mr and Mrs Nail Güreli" written on it. It is not about Nail Güreli. I know him. This is about traditions. I know that he respects women's rights. However, Nazmiye Demirel became Süleyman; Berna Yılmaz became Mesut; Mine Gürel became Nail[14]. If I were them, I would have reacted harshly against it. If these invaluable women reacted against these rules we could go further. (2016, 193)

Tansu Çiller is the first woman Prime Minister in Turkey, and is known for giving her surname to her husband. However, in my interview with lawyer Ayten Ünal, who won the right of first surname usage in the ECHR, she said the following:

> It is not about feminism. We criticised her as feminists, because she did not follow up on this struggle. Her husband went to court before the marriage, and changed his surname of his own volition. Then, when they married, she got his surname, but it was already her surname, so there was no need for a change. She circled back around the law, so it is not a powerful, vivid example.[15] (translated by me)

---

[13] Available at http://sosyal.hurriyet.com.tr/yazar/melis-alphan_350/kadinlara-soyadi-ayrimciligi_40110094 (Accessed: 3 June 2019)
[14] Politicians and their wives' names.
[15] Available at https://www.milliyet.com.tr/pazar/benim-ve-kizim-icin-bir-zafer-151226 (Accessed: 4 June 2019)

"Feminism is the radical notion that women are people" is a popular definition frequently attributed to Cheris Kramarae, Paula Treichler, and Ann Russo; however it first appeared in a feminist newsletter called *New Directions for Women* in 1986 by editor Marie Shear (Jule 2008, 3). Feminism's commitment, as seen in this quote, is achieving the equality of people. Indeed, the notion itself covers all sexes. Thus, the dominant sex that benefits more is investigated. To recap, in my very early experiences at home, I was the one who was apparently less respected than my brother, judged from many angles and not regarded as an individual. Feminism is not a belief that—in my case— my brother should be raised in power above me. In conclusion, I noticed that when the majority of the population is questioning feminism, they are almost supporting the sexism that has been forced on to them by the patriarchal system and its mainstream tools.

Instead of one gender controlling another, accepting everyone as an individual human being might break these labels or even the dichotomy of male and female groups. Why should one group control another? In a modern society, the system is strictly defined even by the colour of toys: Pink versus blue. Those were the very first times we encountered the social ideals of femininity and masculinity. At the end of the day, with no discrimination, feminism is a movement towards equal society for all of us: female, male, transgender people, LGBTIQA+, everyone.

In her article "Women's Movement of the 1980s in Turkey: Radical Outcome of Liberal Feminism", Yeşim Arat (1994) stressed this issue:

On February 4, 1983, Şule Torun addressed the Turkish readers of the weekly literary journal *Somut*[16] with the following argument: The words "woman" and "man" do not reflect anatomical differences. Their meanings are socially constructed and embody differences far beyond the anatomical. Furthermore, these constructed differences create a hierarchy of gender. Consequently, men exploit and women are exploited. (100)

---

[16] A group of professional women prepared a feminist page called *Somut* that represents the seeds of feminist consciousness in Turkey. *Kaktüs*, the first socialist women's review, was first published on 1 May 1988, with the signatures of Sedef Öztürk, Banu Paker, Gülnur Savran, Şahika Yüksel, Nural Yasin, Aksu Bora, Fatmagül Berktay, Nesrin Tura, Özden Dilber, Nalan Akdeniz and Fadime Tonak. Available at http://bianet.org/kadin/siyaset/9780-kaktus-ilk-sosyalist-feminist-dergi (Accessed: 4 June 2019)

As I mentioned in the beginning of this chapter, my early life was heavily influenced by my gender. Eventually, I grew up with these stereotypical gender roles, recognised some of the restrictions, and tried to understand the social, cultural, economic, and religious agendas. Gender is a major part of who we are, and our gender identity—which is socially constructed—shapes our lives, starting from the very first hegemonic regimes in the home.

3.2 From Margin to Centre: Struggling

When I spent time as a volunteer at the Purple Roof Women's Shelter Foundation, I thought I "helped" women there; however, each time without exception, they reciprocally strengthened me. In 1987, feminists put up resistance against male violence for the first time in Turkey. In her article "Feminism in Turkey", Nükhet Sirman discussed the issue:

> In May 1987, about 3000 women marched through the streets of İstanbul to protest against the battering of women in the home. This was not the first time that women in Turkey had taken to the streets, but it certainly was the first time that they had voiced demands specific to their conditions of existence as women in Turkish society. As stated by one of the speakers at the rally marking the end of the march, women were not marching for their nation, their class, nor for their husbands, brothers and sons, but for themselves. (1989, 1)

After that, protests ramped up for solidarity against violence toward women. Women writers gained recognition. Many consecutive campaigns followed such as the Purple Needle Campaign[17] against sexual harassment (Tekeli 1995, 166). Women were saying that they own their own bodies. Women's liberation was gained via these protests. Day by day, women were considered increasingly equal in the system. Subsequently, the collective workbook *Scream So That Everyone Listens / Bağır Herkes Duysun* was published in 1987, based on women's personal experiences. Doctors and lawyers joined the team, creating a solidarity network. In 1989, a telephone help centre was established in order

---

[17] A needle is an accessory and a necessary tool for defence. The first lines of the campaign: "Now I would like to introduce you to a great product. The purple needle you see in my hand is made of a nickel-chrome alloy steel and is 7 cm long. The purple ribbon attached to it makes it an accessory for all of your outfits. I will now show you that this elegant accessory is at the same time a means of defence against anyone molesting you. The movement is this... Stick it in without feeling sorry; do not be afraid, it cannot cause tetanus." Available at http://bianet.org/biamag/kadin/110595-mor-igne-kampanyasi-19-yasinda (Accessed: 4 June 2019)

to minimise domestic violence, and in 1990, the Purple Roof Women's Shelter Foundation was opened and women were further supported (Arat 104).

The Purple Roof Women's Shelter Foundation was significant to me in that I learned subtle types of violence: dating violence, emotional, and verbal abuse. Up until that point, I had thought the only type of violence was the kind with visible results. If I could not see the effects with my eyes, I did not realise that abuse may have occurred. In other words, in a very rigid way, I thought that if there was no blood, there was no violence. Destructing one's self-confidence can indeed be considered major abuse, though. In their article "Violence against Women in Turkey, a Nationwide Survey", Ayşe Gül Altınay and Yeşim Arat speak of a woman named Kardelen, who after severe emotional abuse had trouble remembering her own name.

> Kardelen's story about her name resonates strongly with the bestselling feminist novel *Kadının Adı Yok (The Woman Has No Name)* by Duygu Asena. … [When] Asena died, it was a large group of feminist women who carried her coffin out of the mosque where her funeral prayer had taken place. This was against established religious practice. One large banner said, "The woman has a name. And we will not forget." Kardelen was not at this funeral. She was busy changing her life and the lives of the women around her as one of the very few self-identified feminists in her small town at the Eastern borderlands of Turkey. And it had all begun, quite literally, with remembering and (re)claiming her name. (Altınay and Arat 2009, 8)

When I first went to the foundation, I said "I am going to save women around me" because I had witnessed domestic violence while growing up. Women experts, mostly lawyers and therapists, gave us some needed information and education in the foundation. Moreover, they shared with us statistics, personal experiences, and their expectations. I remember crying silently and leaving the room. Thus, after all that incoming data, I figured out that I could not help women, because I was the one who really needed help in order to survive. On that day, a therapist from the Purple Roof Women's Shelter Foundation, Feride Güneri, gave us a presentation and stressed the point about injured parties and unjustly treated individuals mostly being found in the family home. This brought up not the gender-based differences between my brother and me, but my father's aggression, which reared its head again even after many years had passed. As a result, Güneri was trying to say to me that I was a possible example of a victim of violence, mostly because my father is a man who creates an unstable atmosphere at home with yelling, breaking, pushing, vomiting, and systematic daily torture. Even only this input, that is to say, witnessing it at home, is enough to position one as the aggrieved party when it comes to violence.

At the Purple Roof Women's Shelter Foundation, women's solidarity is empowered, therefore I am a part of it, and that began with my perception of my mother. As the years went by, I questioned social values and women's self-esteem as well as collective processes, with no hierarchical mechanisms and no authorisation. I was in the margins when I was a small kid witnessing domestic violence at home and experiencing gender discrimination. Afterwards, during my struggle, I felt myself moving closer to the centre while communicating with other women, interviewing volunteers, developing my film project, and sharing experiences with others. Psychologically, socially, or legally, the experience exchange empowers everyone. I, as an autoethnographer in this research, follow my own path, my mother's, and other women's as well. The surname change issue is just an aspect of this inequality to come to the surface, and it can be seen as a type of verbal-visual violence in the case of a divorce. Whenever women come across difficulty because of this surname change, it takes a long time for them to push past it.

My journey from margin / from home to centre / Purple Roof Women's Shelter Foundation is a representation of female identity construction, which is not separate from politics. It is worth mentioning the detail of my father's surname being written on our doorbell, and whenever we came home, we saw that surname, supporting his authoritarian position. My autoethnographic film carries clues and reflects back on how daughters will be growing up in the near future as a "second sex". Although women in Turkey are mostly struggling with domestic violence and even murder, I focused on the surname change issue, a subtle violence system that is not readily visible. Whose name is written on your doorbell? When it comes to seeing through the traditionally structured family and its roots, naming conventions might assist to sense the whole picture.

3.3 "The Second Sex" as Other

Simone de Beauvoir, who claims "one is not born, but rather becomes a woman" in *The Second Sex* (1949, 301), relates *The Origin of the Family, Private Property, and the State* by Engels (1978) but catches it shortcomings. According to de Beauvoir, two elements express the woman's position. The first is participation in production. The second is freedom from reproductive slavery. Simone de Beauvoir reckons men oppress women and stresses the boys' privileged position; even at the age of three or four years old they are referred to as "little man" (285-286). She demonstrates that "to ask two spouses bound by practical, social and moral ties to satisfy each other sexually for their whole lives is pure absurdity" (466). Additionally, Simone de Beauvoir says that "marriage is a perverted institution oppressing indeed both men and women" (521). She also thinks that "the goals of wives can be overwhelming as a wife tries to be elegant, a good housekeeper and a good mother" (734). Also, de Beauvoir stresses "the numerous inequalities between a wife and husband" and thinks that "marriage almost always destroys a woman" (518).

As a traditional act, in many societies women usually take on the husband's surname after marriage. His-story tends to be the story of husbands/men and sometimes the agreement starts with name destruction. One is not born with those surnames, but later becomes Mrs Hemingway or Mrs Engels or even Mrs Richard Dalloway, which enables a critical perspective upon the past. In short, hegemonic discourses erase women's voices, lives, rights, and even their habits and names.

3.4 His-story: Marriage as an Identity Crisis

This identity crisis has occurred in a similar way not only in Turkey, but in many countries worldwide. For example, in 1995 94% of British women took their husband's surnames after marriage, according to a Eurobarometer survey (Valetas 2001, 3). In 2013, the proportion was 75%, according to Thwaites' research (2013, 425). In 2014, it was 54%, according to the Discourses of Marriage Research Group's data.[18] Statistically, the ratio is decreasing year by year. Sophie Coulombeau expresses her position in the article "Why Should Women Change Their Names on Getting Married":

> For me, to adopt the surname of my partner and relinquish my own would profoundly affect how I think about my own identity. On the one hand, it would bind us into a family unit and make it easier to know what to write on the birth certificates if we ever have children. But on the other, it would make me first and foremost a wife, while my husband would remain, quite simply, himself. Introducing myself as "Sophie Hardiman" would mean that saying "I do" had fundamentally changed the answer to the question "Who am I?" (2014, 1)

Generally, it is a signal that women obey traditional family rules and become the husband's possession, at least visually on ID cards. Some women think this is important, some not; some of them think that at the end of the day, the

---

[18] Available at https://www.bbc.co.uk/news/magazine-29804450 (Accessed: 21 June 2019)

surname in any case comes from another man—their father—and some think it is meaningless to carry that forward or not. So then what does his-story say? In 1340, one court claims "when a woman took a husband, she lost every surname except 'wife of'" (Coulombeau 2014, 1). Furthermore, jurist Henry de Bracton stresses partners "became a single person, because they are one flesh and one blood" (Coulombeau 2014, 1). By the early 17th century, historian William Camden claims "women with us, at their marriage, do change their surnames, and pass into their husbands' names, and justly. For they are no more twain, but one flesh" (Coulombeau 2014, 1).

On the other hand, feminist and writer Mary Wollstonecraft kept her first surname after a marriage and signed papers as "Mary Wollstonecraft femme [or wife of] Godwin" in 1797 (Mitzi 2003, 160); meanwhile Mary Macarthur and Violent Markham were elected for Parliament with their first surnames (Hamilton 1932, 226). Also, Helena Normanton, the first female barrister in England, got her passport in her first surname in 1924 (Mossman 2014, 451). Moreover, as our names are symbols for our identities and personal integrity, Lucy Stone, a 19th century American woman, signed papers as "Lucy Stone (only)", which can be considered a strong statement for that time period (Bysiewicz and Gloria 1972, 598). Her activist friend Elizabeth Cady Stanton[19] also wrote "nothing has been done in the woman's rights movement for some time that has so rejoiced my heart as the announcement by you of a woman's right to her name. It does seem to me a proper self-respect demands that every woman may have some name by which she may be known from cradle to grave" (Coulombeau 2014, 1).

---

[19] In Elisabeth Griffith's (1984) book *In Her Own Right: The Life of Elizabeth Cady Stanton*, the author mentions about Elizabeth Cady Stanton's name chaos that "the question of how to address the female subjects of biography raises issues of style and substance. Biographers of great men never had to worry about to call their protagonists, who had the same name all their lives. One's subject could age gracefully from 'Young John' to 'Adams' to 'the president' without confusing the reader. Biographers of great women have a more awkward nomenclature if their subject married, or married more than once. How should one address Elizabeth Cady Stanton? Using her first name and nicknames seems juvenile, too familiar, and even disrespectful. Using her family name, Cady, is only appropriate for the period before her marriage, since she did not keep her name as Lucy Stone did. Using her full name is cumbersome but emphatic. For the most part this biography will refer to her as Stanton or Mrs. Stanton, following general newspaper practice. (The New York Times still insists on 'Miss' or 'Mrs.' Always; 'Mr.' is used only for 'men good standing' except on the sport pages.) Her husband Henry will be identified as Mr. Stanton or by using his first name." (Introduction xx)

Lucy Stoners used the motto "my name is my identity and must not be lost" (Coulombeau, 1). Those women used surnames that they preferred, and got their passports, bank accounts and voter registrations in order, although they were viewed as sick, confused, and even "not for a change of name but a competent psychiatrist" (Coulombeau, 1). In 1972, women started to use their first surnames only—if they wanted to—in the US (MacDougall 1971, 2). After those struggles, Sophie Coulombeau gave her free decision on her surname:

> To abandon my surname and take that of my partner would mean abandoning Sophie Coulombeau, along with all the errors, achievements, and resonances she created over thirty years. I would become, first and foremost, my husband's wife. And that is not the whole of me. So I will keep the name Coulombeau. (2014, 1)

3.5 A Surname Reflects a Heritage

Apart from patriarchal customs, there are a lot of reasons for accepting a new surname: being a married couple, rejecting a father's surname or attempting to create a new identity, preferring the husband's surname, or bonding with children. Whatever the reason is, first of all it is an issue with a heterosexist perspective, which assumes that men-men, women-women relationships do not surround us; this is not the reality. Historically names have been used to oppress people, and taking on a husband's surname was a gesture of erasing identity. For example, black people left their African names when forced into slavery. It has been asserted that African-Americans have no knowledge of their family naming traditions. Thus, the last name reflects a heritage that has been conditioned, although "having their names and absolute identities totally taken away upon enslavement left African American slaves almost clueless as to who they were, where they came from and what purpose they served in the earth other than that of abject slavery" (R. Muhammad 2011, 27). The book *Barbershops, Bibles, and Bet: Everyday Talk and Black Political Thought* (2010) stresses the importance of choosing a name that feels right and fitting for the individual, especially for black people who wish to shed the history of slavery:

> Let's say you had a spotted cow in your barn and I lived next door with a spotted cow as well and both looking identical. Say one day you left your gate open and your cow wandered in my barn. And you came over and said, "You got my cow." How would you know which one is yours? ...By the brand. That cow will have your initials branded on him. So, no matter where your cow roams, you will always be able to identify him."

Black people in Hajj's estimation continue to carry the brand or white racists through their "slave names." (Harris-Melissa, Introduction xx)

Also, in the article "Voices of the Condemned: A Comparative Study of the Testimonies of Death Row Exonerees and Slave Narratives" (2014), we come across similar naming practices and the emphasis on the value of "things" rather than "human beings":

Damien Echols' memoir is replete with references to the way in which his identity was destroyed by prison: The whole purpose was to rob everyone of their identity. Dress everyone exactly alike, give them the same haircut, take away their name, and give them a number. To the prison system, I am not Damien Echols. I am inmate SK931. (Malkani 10-11)

Furthermore, slaves had to take on their owners' names, which is another example of dominance over others via the imposition of surnames. Likewise, as is stated in the article "The Long-term Effects of Africa's Slave Trades":

There were a number of ways of identifying the ethnicity or "nation" of a slave. The easiest was often by a slave's name. Slaves were often given a Christian first name and a surname that identified their ethnicity [e.g., Tardieu, 2001]. As well, a slave's ethnicity could often be determined from ethnic markings, such as cuts, scars, hairstyles, or the filing of teeth. [Karasch, 1987, pp. 4–9] (Nunn 2007, 7)

Chapter 4

Documentary

4.1 Putting Things in Motion

Scholars have been utilising documentary film for numerous research purposes such as data collection and data analysis that lead us to question the identity of documentaries. In order to collect credible data, researchers record the interviews. Since it is possible to forget exactly what happened in each moment, the recordings can be used and watched again later on. In the book *Data Collection and Analysis*, Roger Sapsford and Victor Jupp (2006) say the following:

> Not all sources follow the traditional model of written documents: printed text is not the only medium for reproducing words. Modern technologies have made possible the storage and dissemination of sights and sounds other than traditional verbal texts: in radio, for example, film or photographs, and other categories listed under "Images, sound and objects" [...] such as film, photographs, maps, pictures, sound and video recordings. (141)

Academic ethnographers produce documentary films or digital videos in order to assemble, evaluate and share empirical knowledge (MacDougall 2011; Vannini 2015). Some academics have approached film with scepticism due to its subjective structure (Pink 2013; Vannini 2015). Lately, an increasing number of scholars agree on film's momentous potential to highlight social, political and economic issues (Bates 2014; Vannini 2015). Building on the advancement of visual methodologies in the arts and social sciences focuses on many opportunities. The data represent different forms such as visual diaries, mobile gadgets, multi-camera recording, visual ethnography, or ethnographic documentary. By engaging in these disciplines, researchers also discuss equipment, techniques, analysis, and output so as to investigate invisible worlds and offer insights into identity research, everyday life, time, and space.

Documentaries share lives as an innovative cultural form. Rather than just observing, they are also changing the world. It is an audiovisual portrayal of the subjects' way of life. The textures and rhythms of social life in motion, captured even with camera phones at schools or homes, provide new possibilities that video creates within social science. With its sound and movement, video tells us a lot in comparison to sample surveys. For example, the researcher can collect even the mannerisms of the participant, evoking a sense of feeling between spaces and people or animals, things and practices.

When I first applied to the MA programme of the Cinema Department, I already had an idea for a film project. I was going to follow women's stories and their decisions regarding their surname change during their marriages, or even during their divorces. Keeping this project in mind, I took all the relevant courses. Because I graduated from the Visual Arts and Visual Communication Design programme for my BA degree, I thought filming and visualising the topic would be the best option for me, but the implementation was not that easy. On one hand, I believed in my project; on the other hand, I understood that I had to convince other people around me, because filmmaking is a collective process. My reasons for wanting to film came not only from my visual background, but also my desire to create a change in society. As I spent two years at the Filmmor Women's Cooperative, where I was able to contribute films, pursue ideas and act for other women, my involvement in film enhanced my communication skills, and we as women shared an empowered, non-sexist experience. Putting things in motion there was deliberate, and I believe none of our decisions came out of the blue. They were all connected to each other. Such was the case as well with my documentary.

4.2 Filming Part of Yourself

During my MA years, I took the module *Gender, Queer, and the Body in the Aesthetic Expression*[1] from the Cultural Studies Department as an elective, and we watched a documentary in that course called *Mirror Mirror*, by Zamirah Moffat. "It is a documentary based on the audiovisual ethnography of London's queer club Wotever", using dialogues and intersubjectivity.[2] This documentary is part of Moffat's PhD thesis, and she argued that audiovisual participant feedback is an effective process for representation:

> By visual ethnography I mean an ethnography that incorporates the visual not simply as a way of gathering ethnographic data, but as a

---

[1] I would like to thank Dr Cüneyt Çakırlar, our tutor, for the impressive content of the module.
[2] Available at https://loopingthreads.com/2009/04/09/mirror-mirror-by-zamirah-moffat -2006/ (Accessed: 21 June 2019)

device that captures and documents the process of capturing, thereby producing a thoroughly situated knowledge.[3]

Moffat's documentary is a good example of reflection: the filmmaker/researcher reflects on her own presence. Thus, we understand that she films part of herself. After witnessing the process of Moffat's filmmaking experience, I came across Myrdal's commentary on filmmaking:

> In our profession, there is a lack of awareness even today that, in searching for truth, the student, like all human beings whatever they try to accomplish, is influenced by tradition, by his environment, and by his personality. Further, there is an irrational taboo against discussing this lack of awareness. It is astonishing that this taboo is commonly respected leaving the social scientist in naiveté about what he is doing. (1969, 4)

While working on oral history projects, I endeavoured to reveal both the methodology, and myself as a researcher and instrument of data collection. Film is a narrative medium that has a powerful potential in anthropological communication. To see the matter in a new light, take the films of Chantal Akerman, the paintings of Rene Magritte, or the music of John Cage, all of which raise critical consciousness by being openly self-aware and reflexive. "To be reflexive is not only to be self-conscious" (Ruby 2000, 155) but also to know what aspects of self are crucial to an audience.

In this respect, I would like to put an emphasis on Chantal Akerman, the director, and her influence on avant-garde cinema regarding filming part of oneself. When I first watched her *La Chambre* (1972) and *News from Home* (1976), I sent a message to one of my friends/tutors, a film buff, and said, "I met her, Chantal Akerman!" My friend/tutor was thrilled, called me back immediately and asked "How? Where?" Suddenly, I realised that I phrased my sentence incorrectly, because I did not meet Chantal Akerman in person. I felt I was with her during every second of her films that created this influential aura. I did not know her personally; however, it was obvious that she was my intellectual pathfinder who already understood me without saying a word or even adding a personal touch. Her movies created that effect not only on me, but also on Giuliana Bruno, who says in her article "Projection: On Akerman's Screen, From Cinema to the Art Gallery" (2015):

---

[3] Available at https://loopingthreads.com/2009/04/09/mirror-mirror-by-zamirah-moffat -2006/ (Accessed: 21 June 2019)

Chantal Akerman travels across a landscape of images and fashions hybrid artistic spaces as she moves freely between fiction and documentary film and also exhibits work in the art gallery. Since the early 1990s, the celebrated director and writer, who pioneered a new form of cinema in the 1970s, has engaged in expanded ways of screening, in advance of the cultural movement that propels today's filmmakers and artists to exchange roles and work increasingly in between media. Her work challenges the canonical separation between different genres and forms of visual art, for she not only moves back and forth between different kinds of cinema and moving image installation but also finds ways to interchange these modes. (15)

According to Bruno (2016), Akerman captures scenes of everyday life, especially the lives of women. In her movies, physical and mental spaces go hand in hand. A personal story is set, reflection is sensed, and layers create installations. Bruno says that "she speaks clearly of a journey that is a personal geography. [...] Her work always appears to house that memory of someone who is not quite stranger to the places she visits. [...] Her artistic journeys often end up revisiting places close to her own history" (21).

Filmmakers choose whether to keep their own voice in the film or not. Additionally, the perspective of the documentary is generally directed at the "other", which may be distorted by the filters of ideology. Independent documentaries that have no reliance on any institution or sponsor reconstruct the truth with legitimacy as a leading factor. Documentaries have been commonly understood as a real record throughout the ages. Inevitably, even in the process of editing, some include visuals and sound, and some do not. This is shaped by the ideology or aesthetic decisions of the director, writer, and editor—that is to say, several different perspectives. Even from the outside, it is possible to interpret the final output in relation to the person who made the film. Thus, consciousness is appearing in terms of documentaries, and "the other" is not passive, not driven by an authority which is more reflexive and active rather than obedient in autoethnographic films. Not only a personal identity, but also a cultural one can be generated in the process of production of this documentary form. Even in the end, the filmmaker has become "the other".

Feminist film theorist Laura Mulvey's essay "Visual Pleasure and Narrative Cinema", published in 1975, introduces the term "male gaze". In this remarkable article, Mulvey (1989) says that in film, women are "the objects of gaze" (20), and during the '70s, when the essay was written, Hollywood protagonists were mostly heterosexual men. In other words, viewers and producers were overwhelmingly men who were in a position to feature females. For example, even the word "camerawoman" can be evaluated as a reaction to language itself, and also the unbalanced ratio in terms of men versus women in the film sector. Adding women's voices into works of art can solve the crisis of representation. Not only in the film sector, but also in advertising, it is easy to come across brands where the photographer's view of the model expresses "buy the image, get the girl". In postmodern times, the emergence of self-storytellers is increasing. By telling his/her own story, the author or documentary filmmaker challenges the authoritative knowledge of the social world. Especially in this case, if the director is a woman, or African-American, or an LGBTIQA+ individual—that is to say, a member of a disadvantaged group—it can be said that it is more advantageous to narrate the story while keeping in mind Mulvey's gaze—subject/object—definition.

The first-person documentaries are subjective, and have value because the narrators have the chance to tell their own story. First-person narratives can be political or even poetic (Lebow 2012, 1), and depending on the filmmaker, society can adversely be a researcher at certain points. If the filmmaker asks the audience or "the other" to shoot one's own self, the whole story will change. For example, if the filmmaker gives the camera to the viewer and asks to be filmed, the point of view will change and occasionally, the output becomes bidirectional or more sophisticated. As in the Cubist art movement, there are multiple angles and perspectives in first-person documentaries; there are many points of view that render the project more productive and multi-voiced. At this point, I remember Denzin's (2014) words in *Interpretive Autoethnography,* which summarise my position:

> Lives and their experiences, the telling and the told, are represented in stories which are performances. Stories are like pictures that have been painted over, and, when paint is scraped off an old picture, something new becomes visible. What is new is what was previously covered up. A life and performances about it have the qualities of *pentimento.*[4] Something new is always coming into sight, displacing what was previously certain and seen. There is no truth in the painting of a life, only multiple images and traces of what has been, what could have

---

[4] "Pentimento: Something painted out of a picture which later becomes visible again." (Denzin 2014, 1)

been, and what now is. There is no firm distinction between the texts and performances. (1)

4.3 "Cinema of Me"[5] vs. Mainstream Cinema

In the autoethnographic filmmaking or researching process, looking inward, the cinema of me, "documenting I/eye" is considered therapeutic for both the writer and the reader. Especially with issues of gender, class and race, it is nearly a new model of representation of truth and method, which transcends the conflict between the subject and the object. Generally speaking, the subjectivity of "documenting I/eye" constructs a reality out of selected images and sound. If "the documented" are to be covered in an equal power relationship, that will deconstruct hegemonic practices. In mainstream or dominant cinema, the plot is character-led, and usually white, rich, and educated men win, whereas in "autoethnographic documenting I/eye" cases, this changes. Deviants and dissidents might become the main characters. Traditional cinematic codes may be broken before the viewer's eyes. Hollywood's, or locally Yesilçam's dominant system of representation will be shattered. For example, Steven Cohan and Ina Rae Hark discussed this issue in their work entitled *Screening the Male: Exploring Masculinities in Hollywood Cinema* (2012) as follows:

Both within the women's movement and gay movement, there is an important sense in which the images and functions of heterosexual masculinity has been identified as a structuring norm in relation both of images of women and gay men. It has to that extent been profoundly problematised, rendered visible. But it has rarely been discussed and analysed as such. Outside these movements, it has been discussed even less. It is thus very rare to find analyses that seek to specify in detail, in relation to particular films or group of films, how heterosexual masculinity is inscribed and the mechanisms, pressures, and contradictions that inscription may involve. (9)

Dominant cinema represents a natural woman's position as an object rather than a subject. Autoethnographic filmmakers subvert these cinematic codes by looking inside themselves; they are both objects and subjects at the same time and the duality system disappears, because they are hand-in-hand but not facing each other. They make visible what was once invisible. For example,

---

[5] Lebow, Alisa, ed. The Cinema of Me: The Self and Subjectivity in First Person Documentary. London; New York: Wallflower Press, 2012.

anthropologist and filmmaker Moffat's experience is welcoming to her subjects:

> [Their] practice is grounded in the shared anthropological work of ethnographic filmmaker Jean Rouch. In 1974, he placed a call for the audio-visual counter gift as a stimulant for mutual understanding and a route to the heart of knowledge. Rouch's vision parallels that of [their] ethnographic field site. Just as London's newest queer club played host to people of all genders and sexualities, the praxis of shared anthropology heartily welcomes in its subjects. Exploiting the radical nature of the audio-visual counter gift, the intention of this thesis is to convey a new confidence integral to contemporary queer identities, of which [they] have been the privileged beneficiary, witness and host. [6] (ttv-i.net 2013, 1)

The most significant prototypes of first-person films belong to Jean Rouch. There are other early first-person works, such as Amalie Rothschild's *Nana, Mom and Me* (1974) and Michele Citron's *Daughter Rite.* (1978) Moreover, some of Agnès Varda's documentaries like *Uncle Yanco* (1967) and *Daguerrèotypes* (1976) can be counted as strong pieces for displaying the filmmaker's subjective gaze. Bearing in mind these examples, age, gender, race, class, and sexuality affect both reception and meaning in production. Looking into oneself is an honest way to document; however, there also needs to be a distance perspective, to an extent where it is probably not possible that self is the observer. In dominant ideology, and reflectively in mainstream cinema, the man is gazing at the woman. The spectator imitates this. One's eye looking at itself can break the voyeuristic pleasure of the mainstream "documenting eye" apparatus. As a result, the "documenting eye" and the output are joined together and obviously transcend the conflict between subject and object, which in turn raises the question of what need and whose need it fulfils. In classic narrative cinema, men are the subjects and women are the objects, like black and white, nature and culture, East and West. In this construct, the female is passive and the object of male desire.

Additionally, motion and emotion, visual and tactile, or optic and haptic approaches can be discussed, which might be eye-opening and assist in comprehending the issue as a whole when it comes to moving image and bipolarities. Haptic theories appeared in Giuliana Bruno's book *Atlas of Emotion: Journeys in Art, Architecture, and Film* (2002), where we came across

---

[6] Available at http://www.ttv-i.net/?p=1534 (Accessed: 21 June 2019)

Alois Riegl's notion of the haptic. (247) For Riegl, the haptic involves "the presence of representational flatness and planarity". (250) Furthermore, Walter Benjamin subverted the distinction between haptic and optic. In the *Atlas of Emotion*, Margaret Iversen emphasises the issue:

> The modern "tactile" mode of perception involves a challenge to the senses. [...] Benjamin's appreciation of Riegl's theory did not prevent him from turning it upside down that is by making modern perception tactile or haptic rather than optic. (250)

Giuliana Bruno, on the other hand, says (2002) that film takes us to another place in the here and now, as evidenced by Sugimoto, a Japanese-born photographer who lives in New York and Tokyo:

> The photographer explores his subjects serially, looking into images analytically and connecting them panoramically. Once related to one another in their endless variations, and to all the other series, the pictures articulate, almost, literally, a film series. The dioramic seriality takes shape as a unique cinematic project. [...] This is an emotional topography that takes place within the architectural transport of the movie "house". Cinema is indeed a house: home of voyages, architecture of the interior, it is a map of cultural travel. (52)

These cinematic projects or voyages of film images usually form the entirety of the sensation. From my point of view map of cultural travel, "the individual 'I' does not exist alone, but with 'another'" (Lebow 2012, 2).

Giuliana Bruno (2002) points out that critical concern can move away from the pictorial object, and that visual arts can be perceived as agents in the making of space. In adopting the emotional viewpoint for architecture or film viewing, the viewer has to transform their sense of those art forms.

> By working to conceive a methodological practice that is "in between", we aim to corrode the opposition between immobility-mobility, inside-outside, private-public, dwelling-travel, and to unloose the gender boxing and strictures these oppositions entail. [...] A frame for cultural mapping, film is modern cartography. It is a mobile map—a map of differences, a production of socio-sexual fragments and cross-cultural travel. Film's site-seeing—a voyage of identities in transit and a complex tour of identifications—is an actual means of exploration: at once a housing for and tour of our narrative and our geography. (71)

4.4 Creating Narration, Directing Documentary

At first, my aim was to express a personal but political issue by using film language. While in the preproduction process, I found myself creating a hypothesis that "men dominate and force surnames on women at the time of marriage". Thus, I was going to get outside the system and collect my proof, data, and people. I wrote a proposal, then researched, then made a presentation; however, some people did not believe in or understand the project. This is because some of them have no idea about feminism although they are women, and some of them believed in other projects that they found more important. Determined, I continued outlining observations, capturing clear sound, producing the camerawork, editing smooth transitions, and getting feedback again and again.

Finding people to interview is not an easy task. Sometimes distance was a barrier; other times, subjects were busy and did not have time. Although I had a full-time job and was attending my MA courses at the same time, I managed to create a suitable environment for the project. I used my holidays to shoot. In the end, I arranged a meeting with a feminist professor who was willing to tell her story. Unfortunately, I could not use the footage in the final product; it was my very first interview, and I only realised later that the video was shaky and the audio could not be heard. Before that day, I had never used a camera own my own, and I learned that it was a very difficult task to record, interview, and monitor the sound all on my own. So although my subject's story was striking, I could not use it. This is one aspect of the issues that affected my documentary. Another is the ethical concern. Not only I did not use those clips, but also I neglected to inform my interviewee that I would not be using her story in my project. When I sent the output to festivals, one of our common contacts reported that she was hurt, or felt used for nothing, or had other negative feelings about the experience. Thus, I learned from that communication that we as researchers or filmmakers owe certain things to our interviewees.

A Canon Vixia HF S100 was my primary camera, with a little feathered microphone on it. Before I got that camera, I was allowed to use the other available cameras, which were so huge that I could not carry them. I did try to use them, but the result was much frustration. In the end, I bought a camera that I could carry around with me. I shot my film in 2012, and I did not use a telephone camera either, because there were none available to me. Eventually, I succeeded in buying a camera on an instalment plan. I learned that technical difficulties might stand in the way, and I had to come up with workarounds. Indeed, obstacles popped up frequently, and the only recourse was to be self-assertive. Holding the audience's attention was the top priority.

The first scene in my documentary is a powerful real-life shot which includes harshness directed at me from my ex-husband. That is the only scene that I shot with his telephone. Because of the technical quality gap between a professional camera and a telephone, one of the film festivals called me to ask if there had been some mistake. Regarding this choice—using the telephone's built-in recorder—it was my conscious decision to keep the footage because of its narrative strength. Other visuals and scenes were recorded with the Canon.

As supporting material, I researched some famous scenes from Godard's movie *Weekend* (1967) and related scenes from a popular TV series entitled *Sex and the City* (1998-2004). Although these samples are keenly different from each other in terms of their production dates, they are similar in their intended audience and the visual language they suggest. As a viewer, I watched both types and found them both enriching. One of them is a tough Godard film while the other is a popular TV series; however, for both audiences, the message is the same in terms of the surname issue. My aim was to reach as large an audience as possible, hence why I kept both of them. By doing that, I demonstrated that my topic, the question of surname issue, is a debate that goes back to the '60s and exists in a diverse array of genres. Also, I used flying birds to represent freedom, flue gas images to represent suffocation, and my feet struggling in the sand and my hair as an abstract shadow in order to evoke emotion, to try to break the monotony of the "talking head" so common in documentaries.

During the process, I talked to many people, including some in Parliament. Initially, I planned to interview only women and homosexuals, but not heterosexual men. My reason was obvious to me; I did not want to hear them at all, because in our daily lives, they have the opportunity to express their feelings and thoughts ubiquitously. Afterwards, I clarified this issue with my advisor, Nurşen Bakır, who encouraged me to talk with heterosexual men as well. I did not like the idea at first, but gave it a try. At the end of the research, in collecting the data, I realised that those were the scenes that demonstrated the entirety of the tension. I saw the value, contrast, and conflict and put those stories in the film. Unconsciously, I did not use heterosexual men's images in my documentary, but only their voices. By doing this, I gave the visibility to women and people in the LGBTIQA+ community. On the other hand, I questioned the issue by keeping their voices. Additionally, my voice and questions are dominant as a filmmaker, which helps the audience comprehend the whole. I know by experience that the camera's presence changes the course of a story, and as such, I strive to use it in an appropriate form. Incidentally, each time I heard my voice in the editing process, as I was the editor, I felt alienated. At the end of the filmmaking process, I came to the conclusion that my hypothesis was not correct. Not every man dominates his wife in terms of the surname issue—only some of them do. Men also have some difficulties in the patriarchal system.

When I saw the results, I was really shocked, and thanked my advisor for putting me on the path toward asking the other side of the story. Significantly, making documentaries means you are learning about yourself. The authors of *Art and Fear* point out that

> the only work really worth doing—the only works you can do convincingly—is the work that focuses on the things you care about. To not focus on those issues is to deny the constants in your life. (Bayles and Orland 2001, 116)

After the documentary was completed it was selected and screened in film festivals and conferences, including but not limited to the 2nd International Crime and Punishment Film Festival, the 2nd International Feminist Forum, the 3rd International Accessible Film Festival, the 6th İstanbul Documentary Days/Documentarist, the 9th International Akbank Short Film Festival, the 11th International Filmmor Women Film Festival, and the 16th International Flying Broom Film Festival. Additionally, national newspapers and column writers featured my film and discussed its effects in outlets such as Bianet, Hayat TV, IMC TV, *Milliyet*, NTV, *Radikal*, T24, TRT and *Vatan*. As a student film with no budget, it fulfilled the criteria, and I graduated from university with happiness, gratitude, and a documentary. Afterward, I got divorced, started my PhD, and published a book about mistresses[7]—that is to say, the ones who are unseen in relationships. However, the focus was once again on family structures. As a result, I am moving forward. Although there are new amendments regarding the surname issue in Turkey, nowadays I have somewhat lost interest in the topic. To conclude, watching documentaries prepares us to take action; however, sometimes making them leaves us with little else to say.

4.5 Representing Reality

Does a good documentary stimulate discussion about its subjects, not itself? How crucial is the form? Is it all about meaning and values? Here is Plato's view:

---

[7] The book's Turkish title is *Ne Zaman Boşanacaksın da Evleneceğiz?* (2015), which means *When Are You Going to Divorce and We Get Married?* and it strikes a responsive chord among the audience.

When the mind's eye is fixed on objects illuminated by truth and reality [the sun], it understands and knows them, and its possession of intelligence is evident; but when it is fixed on the twilight world of change and decay, it can only form opinions, its vision is confused and its opinions shifting, and it seems to lack intelligence. (Nichols 1991, 3)

What is the relation between image and reality? In this respect, in *The Evil Demon of Images and the Precession of Simulacra*, Baudrillard says the following:

The secret of the image [...] must not be sought in its differentiation from reality, and hence in its representative value (aesthetic, critical or dialectical), but on the contrary in its "telescoping" into reality. For us, there is an increasingly definitive lack of differentiation between image and reality which no longer leaves room for representation as such [...] There is a kind of primal pleasure, of anthropological joy in images, a kind of brute fascination unencumbered by aesthetic, moral, social or political judgments. It is because of this that I suggest they are immoral, and that their fundamental power lies immorality. (Nichols 1991, 6)

Is reality composed in the shadows? Is it an only imitation, or copies of the copy? Metaphors and abstraction create deeper meaning. Furthermore, reality is collapsed in the surface of simulations. Here, my approach is close to Michael Haneke's concept of the lie of reality or the realistic illusion of film, which is self-referential exploration. In *The Paris Review*, Haneke (2014) says that he hopes his films provoke reflection, and that in turn, he recognises that they could have a political effect. His view is that ideologies are inherently uninteresting from an artistic standpoint, to the extent that they can kill the artistic vibrancy of a piece. After all, if an artwork can be described in a single concept, then there is no depth, no conflict, and no artistic merit. He goes on to admit that although political convictions can seep into artwork, they have to be approached with an air of self-awareness:

At the academy, I always lecture on propagandistic films of various origins so as to sensitise my students to their particular way of functioning. [...] My objective is a humanistic one—to enter into a dialogue with my viewers and to make them think. There is not much more you will be able to achieve in the dramatic arts. And frankly, I don't know what else you should be able to achieve. [...] We live in an age of media ubiquity and it is good to inspire doubts in the viewer as to our supposed "reality." That, at least, is what I have set out to do. Only bad films provide answers and explanations for everything. (5)

Keeping in mind all these views, in my documentary, there is a part where I am saying "nothing" despite vocalising. I use "nothing" here, because in our daily language, every word embraces a meaning and we reach an agreement with the help of words, although we do not all get the same understanding from those words. We perceive differently. Thus, even though we use words, sometimes they are wasted on someone. At first, I wrote down the sentences that I wanted to share. After that, I took out the vowels—which help us to read—from the sentences and I struggled to read the text. The output was "Mmppttkkll [...] Rrryyvvnm [...] Ttkkhhfff". If you attempt to read all the consonants without vowels, you will encounter a certain abstraction that creates a sensation. In conclusion, instead of only explaining the mechanics of the issue, I rather demonstrated it through abstract vocalising, and the result is composed of odd sounds, struggling reflections, and meaning in the meaningless, which represents my reflection and reality.

Chapter 5

Participatory Culture

5.1 Spreadability: My Story Is (Y)ours

At the beginning of this final chapter, I would like to highlight and conclude how the experience of participatory culture hones the primary output, that is to say, my documentary's distribution journey. Before doing that, I would like to mention my articles "Autoethnography as Documentary: My Story is (Y)ours", which was presented at San Angelo University (2013), and "Mrs Private Property", which was presented in Prague (2013) and published in the book *All Equally Real / Femininities Masculinities Today* under the chapter *The Personal is the Political: Femininities and Masculinities in Socio-Political Contexts* by Inter-Disciplinary Press Oxford, United Kingdom (2014). I also presented my developed article, after collecting a variety of feedback from those scholars and editors I met with, in a media conference called *Dijital Sınırlar ve Temsiliyet / Digital Boundaries and Representation* (2013) at İstanbul Bilgi University. I did not imagine at first that I was writing my thesis by interacting with those communities in person. Those entire "hard-wired" connections formed the agenda, making me ready to open out to an "online" media.

Participatory culture argues that power on online participatory platforms includes open-endedness (Langlois 2013, 91). In a networked culture, we spread information—consciously or otherwise—via social media tools such as Facebook, Twitter, Friendster, MySpace, YouTube channels, and game clans. In my case, I have consciously made the decision and produced a documentary, which is telling my story as well as others', with a visual communication and cultural studies background. It is worth sharing with others, as everybody has a surname, where it created an environment in which people spoke up, and in some cases, changed their opinions. Spreadable media[1] focuses on cultural

---

[1] *Spreadable Media: Creating Value and Meaning in a Networked Culture* is a book written by Henry Jenkins, Sam Ford and Joshua Green, in which they discussed the term. Thus, "Henry Jenkins coined the term 'participatory culture' to describe the cultural production and social interactions of fan communities, initially seeking a way to differentiate the activities of fans from other forms of spectatorship." (19)

practices, and discusses why sharing is an effective tool or creates a domino effect. Digital media, which I used frequently during my documentary's distribution process, provided a reimagining of social and political participation. For instance, Henry Jenkins, Sam Ford, and Joshua Green use terms such as "spread", "spreadable", or "spreadability" to define media circulation, and this concept assists our collective conversation.

My research offers a way of conceptualising social media as a system of elements using both digital and traditional media, and highlights a case study of efforts to reach a significant audience. Keeping in mind that in a world where "one-third of teens share what they create online with others, 22 percent have their own web sites, 19 percent blog, and 19 percent remix online content" (Jenkins 2009, 3), with one click I could communicate with almost anyone I wanted to, and very quickly. During that sharing process, people around me from Generation Y advised that I should only send the link to professionals. I did not listen to them because I agreed with Henry Jenkins, Sam Ford, and Joshua Green, who say in their book *Spreadable Media: Creating Value and Meaning in a Networked Culture* that, "our message is simple and direct: if it does not spread, it is dead" (2013, 18).

In *Confronting the Challenges of Participatory Culture* by Henry Jenkins, participatory culture is defined as one with:

> Relatively low barriers to artistic expression and civic engagement, strong support for creating and sharing creations with others, some type of informal mentorship whereby what is known by the most experienced is passed along to novices, members who believe that their contributions matter, [and] members who feel some degree of social connection with one another (at the least, they care what other people think about what they have created). (2009, 22)

Participatory culture transfers the spotlight of literacy from one's declaration to society's involvement. During that time, cultural, informational, and semiotic flows of meaning shape the process, which affects the user's perception. Although the barrier to artistic expression is defined as low in terms of sharing, the documentary production process was not effortless. Nowadays, filming the content with nonstop scenes via iPhones, and sharing it with a click in seconds in 3G / 4G / 5G environments, is the norm. My experience was very different in 2012: the "old" production way of filmmaking that met with "new" distribution channels. In having these experiences and media literacy, I believe that eventually—given the possibility of spreadability and circulation of meaning—my story became (y)ours.

I learned that in participatory culture, while we are consuming (watching) the product (documentary), we are also contributing (sharing), and as a result, we are reproducing it. By telling and sharing our stories, the message is "transformed into the content of an expression—an empty form to which various possible senses can be attributed" (Eco 1984, 5). Each party touches the message and gives a new shape to the initial output. The message is constantly changing during the process, depending on the receiver's experience or point of view. That is what I understand of multi-voices and multi-perspectives. The crucial element here is to separate the discussions on the surface, the dialogue itself. Furthermore, as Jenkins (2009) said, "our focus here is not on individual accomplishment but rather the emergence of a cultural context that supports widespread participation in the production and distribution of media" (4). Remarkably, I used new media in order to reach old media. A report on *The Future of Independent Media* argued this about cultural transformation:

> The media landscape will be reshaped by the bottom-up energy of media created by amateurs and hobbyists as a matter of course. This bottom-up energy will generate enormous creativity, but it will also tear apart some of the categories that organise the lives and work of media makers. A new generation of media-makers and viewers are emerging which could lead to a "sea change" in how media is made and consumed [...] This report celebrates a world in which everyone has access to the means of creative expression and the networks supporting artistic distribution. The Pew study suggests something more: young people who create and circulate their own media are more likely to respect the intellectual property rights of others because they feel a greater stake in the cultural economy [...] We are moving away from a world in which some produce and many consume media toward one in which everyone has a more active stake in the culture that is produced. (Jenkins 2009, 11-12)

While sharing my film, I had no idea about this "sea change" feedback process, and how it supported forward-thinking. Moreover, as Jenkins (2009) stated "the new media literacy should be seen as social skills, as ways of interacting within a larger community, and not simply as individualised skills to be used for personal expression" (32). The receivers are the ones who watched my documentary via film festivals, or the independent viewers who clicked a link through the internet to reach the content or message. In diversified experiences, "audiences [receivers] act as 'multipliers' who attach new meaning to existing properties, as 'appraisers' who evaluate the worth of different bids on our attention, as 'lead users' who anticipate new markets for newly-released content, as 'retro curators' who discover forgotten content" (Jenkins, Ford, Green 2013, 297). Also, Aaron Delwiche and Jennifer Jacobs Henderson (2012) mention Pierre Lévy's vision regarding democratic structures in their article "What is Participatory Culture" as follows:

> Pierre Lévy identified the existence of a "universally distributed intelligence, constantly enhanced, coordinated in real time, and resulting in the effective mobilisation of skills" (13). Pointing out that "no one knows everything" and "everyone knows something", Lévy argued that it was now possible to create democratic political structures in which people could participate directly as unique individuals rather than as members of undifferentiated mass. (6)

Thus, in the last stage, the feedback phase, the audience who watched my film shared their own stories, and dynamically completed the communication from an individual to a group, and we obtained knowledge together.

5.2 The Death of the Author: Long Live the New Dandelions

The internet has transformed our lives over the past ten years. Information spreads quickly. Possibilities are enhanced. Classic methods are replaced by new ones.

Since this is the new status quo, I shared a link to my documentary with columnists I did not know in person. I found their email addresses in the newspapers they write for, sent messages, informed them about my documentary, and asked whether they would find it an appropriate topic about which to write. In the article "Think Like a Dandelion", author Cory Doctorow (2016) correlates this process of sharing to a dandelion spreading its seeds. In the example of the dandelion—new media—we do not know where the process ends. We are experiencing creative methods. In addition, viewers share their comments or subjects for their own purposes.

Doctorow (2016) also gives the example of mammals and their relation to old media, pointing out that mammals spend a lot of time and energy keeping track of their offspring, because of the preciousness and magnitude of the investment. For those who do, unfortunately suffer the loss of a child, the extent of the grief can be so great that some never recover from it fully. This is, of course, in stark contrast to how plant reproduction works:

A single dandelion may produce 2,000 seeds per year, indiscriminately firing them off into the sky at the slightest breeze, without any care for where the seeds are heading and whether they'll get a hospitable reception when they touch down. [...] And indeed, most of those thousands of seeds will likely fall on hard, unyielding pavement, there to lie fallow and unconsummated, a failure in the genetic race to survive and copy. [...] Dandelions and artists have a lot in common in the age of the internet. If you blow your works into the net like a dandelion clock on the breeze, the net itself will take care of the copying costs. (1)

That route may seem an easy one; however, when it comes to communication, accordingly, I refuse to act "hard-wired", and my "dandelion" method worked with its seeds. For example, Asu Maro, who writes for *Milliyet*— one of the popular mainstream newspapers—saw the seeds of my effort and commented on my documentary:

Hande Çayır's documentary summarises the surname issue in a stupendous way. It all starts with not accepting the dismissive reaction of others, like "leave the surname issue alone, and similar stuff, as well." [...] I watched the short documentary recently. In the very first moment, the movie prompts anger due to the opening dialogue between a man and a woman. We are in the dark, in a car, and do not see their faces. We understand that the woman is a director, mentioning her new project. [...] The man answers that "it is kind of ridiculous, my love". We understand in that moment that he is her boyfriend or husband. He says "my love"; however, he has no interest in the topic on which his love decided to make a film. [...] If one person is struggling with one topic that much, it is important for her. At first, we have to understand this. If one would like to keep her first surname, which was with her from birth, and see that as a component part of her identity, no one has the right to take that surname from her.[2] (translated by me)

Although Maro's comments totally overlapped mine, I sent her a second email explaining that my ex-husband was a very nice person, and how he actually helped my film. However, I added at the end of the email that "you might be right, because my documentary also agrees with you". It is weird that even after a divorce, I could accept neither his behaviour nor my passive reactions. This

---

[2] Available at http://www.milliyet.com.tr/cadde/asu-maro/kadinlar-gemi-aziya-aldi-1682052 (Accessed: 4 June 2019)

was powerful feedback for me, to look back over my communication style and my honest act. Thus, Maro states above about my ex-husband that "he says 'my love'; however, he has no interest in the topic on which his love decided to make a film". She got that impression because I created the film like that. Later, when I came across her opinion in the newspaper, I became alienated from my own position and remembered Umberto Eco's words in his work with Stefan Collini, entitled *Interpretation and Overinterpretation* (1992):

> The response of the author must not be used in order to validate the interpretations of his text, but to show the discrepancies between the author's intention and the intention of the text. [...] There can be, finally, a case in which author is also textual theorist. In certain cases [s]he can say, "No, I did not mean this, but I must agree that the text says it, and I thank the reader that made me aware of it". Or, "Independently of the fact that I did not mean this, I think that a reasonable reader should not accept such an interpretation, because it sounds uneconomical". (73)

Although I felt alienated after facing these thoughts and comments, I destroyed and reconstructed myself, like in the film editing process, finally arriving at a place of complete acceptance. In the feedback process, facing the opinions of others strengthens the construction. No further intention exists outside my text or documentary. I learned to respect the latest output/text/documentary. Umberto Eco (1984) also discusses the author's intention in his work:

> My idea of textual interpretation as the discovery of a strategy intended to produce a model reader, conceived as the ideal counterpart of a model author (which appears only as a textual strategy), makes the notion of an empirical author's intention radically useless. We have to respect the text, not the author as person so-and-so. (66)

Müge İplikçi, writer and academician from *Vatan*, watched my film online and shared her interpretation in her column, which was a surprise for me. Although I did not know these people in person, they reacted to the link I sent, and shared their comments. In the book *Interpretation and Overinterpretation*, Umberto Eco (1992) describes the dilemma between the reader's interpretation and writer or content creator:

> When I write a theoretical text I try to reach, from a disconnected lump of experiences, a coherent conclusion and I propose this conclusion to

my readers. If they do not agree with it, or if I have the impression that they have misinterpreted it, I react by challenging the reader's interpretation. When I write a novel, on the contrary, even though starting (probably) from the same lump of experiences, I realise that I am not trying to impose a conclusion: I stage a play of contradictions. (140)

Although I am not aware of these content creators' dilemmas at that period of time, and I did not impose a conclusion in my documentary, İplikçi interprets the film in the same way that I do:

Becoming everyone but not yourself... This sentence covers the internalised roles of women, as well as internalised male roles, and when we realise how this defines our lives, I suppose the reality of the situation is slowly revealed. In any case, it is certainly squared away in the context of the film.[3] (translated by me)

In addition, İnci Tulpar from *Posta* newspaper wrote about my film and remained neutral:

I would especially like to recommend a short film directed by Hande Çayır, entitled *Yok Anasının Soyadı / Mrs His Name*. The documentary is about women changing their surnames when they get married or divorced. The theme is processed in every aspect, from a name written on a doorbell to lost IDs in government offices.[4] (translated by me)

Although male writers[5] did not write about my film, after a conference in the US, a man approached me and asked about the harm to the children when divorced parents insist on keeping or changing their surnames. As opposed to the others, this feedback was not digital, but rather a precious face-to-face encounter. In this process, I was collecting even the tiniest feedback so as to hone my work. Through this, I realised that I prefer face-to-face communication where the dialogue flows, and it is usually more sincere.

---

[3] Available at http://www.gazetevatan.com/muge-iplikci-522341-yazar-yazisi-kendine-gel/ (Accessed: 5 June 2019)

[4] Available at http://m.posta.com.tr/Yazar-Yazisi/170041 (Accessed: 5 June 2019)

[5] On the other hand, Kaos GL, a dedicated LGBTIQA+ community, invited me to present my film at the second Feminist Forum in Ankara.

At first, I mentioned the psychological effects and the possibility of stigma at school. When children or teachers realise that a kid's surname is different from her/his mother's, they have a tendency to judge the child. After my presentation, the man told me about his fiancée, who is a divorced woman. She and her kids have the same surname, which is not common after a divorce; however, in this example, this second prospective husband was putting pressure on her to take his own surname. If she were to the new husband's surname, then her kids' surname would be different from hers. This man told me that his fiancée even cried over the surname issue. He also added that in the US, the equal rights system is different from Turkey's legal situation; however, he made me understand once again that it is not only a problem of legal rights, but a social issue as well. His fiancée has every legal right to keep her surname if they marry; however, this man was attempting to dominate her and the kids socially and psychologically. His voice faded out, but only after he said he would not twist her arm anymore, because he now understood what the harm was. Although I never saw that man again, I carry his words with me even now. In my surreal world, I believed that I touched this man's emotional life through my presentation. At the end of the day, I called this incident a change.

Nonetheless, turning back to online comments, those made in the Ekşi Sözlük (an online dictionary, literally "Sour Dictionary") under the nickname Lacivert Kadife ve Kırmızı Vişne (Prussian Blue Velvet and Red Morello) depicted my documentary as coming out of nowhere, almost like a sniper:

> The documentary opens a door related to existentialism, and if one watches it with a desire to know one's own self without isolating from society, and then it carries meaning. With its sincerity and with the variety of different people interviewed, with symbolic narration, and with a jazzed-up editing method, the film is not a didactic one. By prompting oneself to ask the question "who are those people", it becomes a visual-cultural product. I particularly like the very old lady[6] who says with insensitivity that if she had the same brain in those days that she has now, she would not marry.[7] (translated by me)

Another user on the Ekşi Sözlük, using the nickname Polly Jean, shared the following:

---

[6] She died during the writing of this research.

[7] Available at https://eksisozluk.com/yok-anasinin-soyadi--3270458 (Accessed: 4 June 2019)

It is striking. It is very clear. If it is watched in conjunction with a book entitled *Tarihin Cinsiyeti / The Gender of History* from Fatmagül Berktay[8] it will be very well understood. Thank you, Hande Çayır. It is indeed the exact summary of our problem. Whenever someone is interested in women's issues, she will always hear prohibitive words.[9] (translated by me)

In the end, there was no negative comment at all; however, I am not sure if some part of society ignored the film or not. As Christine Romans said, "many are making a social statement by not joining"[10] (CNN 2009, 1). It seems that we are communicating something about ourselves via our refusal. Indeed, the spectator selects the information or emotion that matches his or her personal baggage. Additionally—and especially—in the reportage, I noted that my own sentences were rarely published without changes. They became the reader's new output, but not mine anymore. Usually, I came across totally new sentences, passed off as mine, but with a different meaning. This is a kind of communication barrier, or is "the death of the author". I came to the conclusion that it is almost impossible to be completely understood, or that the process inevitably gets out of control. If we are understood completely, do we still pursue the dialogue? In addition, the need of being understood drops a hint for another research topic. It might be a boring one though, as the focal point is not plural, but singular, i.e., the self. Moreover, the value here can be defined with new social dynamics of engagement, cultural production and consumption. The value is generated via spreadability, which resonates in our culture by taking on new meanings, creating new values, and even finding a new audience.

At that point, in remembering Roland Barthes's poststructuralist titular catchphrase in *The Death of the Author*[11], he emphasises this communication dilemma:

Let us return to Balzac's sentence: no one (that is, no "person") utters it: its source, its voice is not to be located; and yet it is perfectly read; it is

---

[8] Professor Berktay has done important work in the field, and wrote a PhD thesis entitled *Women and Religion: Discourses of Domination and Resistance*. This study was published as *Tek Tanrılı Dinler Karşısında Kadın* (1996) and was published in English as *Women and Religion* (1998).

[9] Available at https://eksisozluk.com/yok-anasinin-soyadi--3270458 (Accessed: 1 June 2019)

[10] Available at http://edition.cnn.com/2009/TECH/07/01/facebook.holdouts/?iref= nextin (Accessed: 21 June 2019)

[11] The phrase represents the poststructuralist dismissal of the author.

because the true locus of writing is reading. [...] In this way is revealed the whole beginning of writing: a text consists of multiple writings, issuing from several cultures and entering into dialogue with each other, into parody, into contestation; but there is one place where this multiplicity is collected, united, and this place I not the author, as we have hitherto said it was, but the reader. (2001, 6)

To recap, Roland Barthes said that "the author is dead". Cory Doctorow said "dandelions and artists have a lot in common in the age of the internet".[12] In this age, in our community, we are together creating a text; someone starts, others add on. Indeed, everyone is as a whole becoming the author. The content is shaped again and again, sometimes converging to the original meaning, and sometimes diverging. The latest meaning depends on the latest intervention. The meaning is altered, grows, and dies like dandelions. In my documentary process, the other authors around me played with the original material—plasticine—by sharing their points of view. At that point, I saw that there was more than one author. The process resembles this definition of Joseph Kosuth's representation of a chair three ways, in his well-known work of art *One and Three Chairs* at The Museum of Modern Art (MoMa):

[...] as a manufactured chair, as a photograph, and as a copy of a dictionary entry for the word "chair". The installation is thus composed of an object, an image, and words. Kosuth did not make the chair, take the photograph, or write the definition; he selected and assembled them together. Which representation of the chair is most accurate? These open-ended questions are exactly what Kosuth wanted us to think about when he said that "art is making meaning". By assembling these three alternative representations, Kosuth turns a simple wooden chair into an object of debate and even consternation, a platform for exploring new meanings.[13]

Thus, if readers create the meaning, and if my documentary is the manufactured chair, and if one of the respondents—let's say Ekşi Sözlük (Sour Dictionary)[14] writers—create a dictionary definition or textual feedback to my

---

[12] Available at https://craphound.com/context/Cory_Doctorow_-_Context.pdf (Accessed: 21 June 2019)

[13] Available at http://www.moma.org/learn/moma_learning/joseph-kosuth-one-and-three-chairs-1965 (Accessed: 4 June 2019)

[14] "Ekşi Sözlük is a collaborative 'dictionary' based on the concept of Web sites built up on user contribution." (Wikipedia)

documentary, which one is the most accurate? Although my documentary does not have four legs like a chair, I agree with the idea that the essential part here is to create a platform, an atmosphere, or waves for exploring new meanings, and we are like dandelions that may produce many seeds.

5.3 Selfie Age: A Museum without Walls

Media are continually reproducing and replacing themselves, that is to say, media need their functional tools in order to survive. Online identities are being created performatively in this particular medium; private experiences are being shared in an arbitrary way by the help of technology's speed. In addition, selfies[15] sometimes opt for some ads, and become part of them. Moreover, in the contemporary arena, these strategies can be altered: digital art installations, theme parks, malls, and so forth.

Digital mobile social media literacy has created the i-Generation, including social friends, digital personas, and public Wi-Fi spaces. At some point, this game becomes similar to the movie *The Truman Show* (1998), which can be considered a kind of delusion. Alternatively, social transformation in what we call postmodernism narrates its own forms; this is evident in online activism via blogs, virtual communities and personal reputation management systems, career development via LinkedIn plus social recruiting activities, and social background checks. In this online hub, the process is non-linear, spontaneous, reactive, and creating the basis for information gathering. It is interactive, virtual and fragmented. Although the viewer can control the individual sequences, as with virtual reality, the bigger picture is commanded by something else. Every single click a user makes, or sites visited regularly, credit payments processed via online access, or educational information updated on Facebook, are all gathered under the heading of big data (Zikopoulos and Chris 2011).

The entertainment industry has taken a keen interest in this as well. Reality becomes almost pornographic through these lenses. On one hand, does Big Brother continuously watch us? The answer might be yes, as evidenced when ads for products we like interestingly and suddenly appear while we are

---

[15] "We live in the age of the selfie. A fast self-portrait, made with a smartphone camera and immediately distributed into a network, is an instant visual communication of where we are, what we're doing, who we think we are, and who we think is watching. Selfies have changed aspects of social interaction, body language, self-awareness, privacy, and humour, altering temporality, irony, and public behaviour. It's become a new visual genre—a type of self-portraiture formally distinct from all others in history. Selfies have their own structural autonomy." (Saltz 2014, 1)

searching. As its own providers form the social media community, Google also provides a variety of information about its users for advertisers. These ads are often sold in cost-per-click, and the revenue becomes larger and larger each day, in regular proportion to the number of users. It is emotionally connected, that is to say, each individual's psychology becomes an output for this big revenue. On the other hand, as Henry Jenkins states in an HCD Media Group video[16], "we instead with a cell phone cameras are watching Big Brother moment of the day". Likewise, we do not watch much TV anymore, but our TV is watching us. We are carrying a newer version of a TV in our pockets. In his TED talk[17], Jenkins also emphasises that "young people do things in the world that matter. Young people can take responsibility and change the world around them. Young people are social agents. Young people need space to pursue those interest and those interests need to be taken seriously". After witnessing all these developments, especially the vloggers I follow[18], I cannot devote myself in the future solely to documentary forms of production, as museums have no walls anymore; yet we have internet communication.

Presently, as we are living in the age of selfies, using oneself as data is—by the help of autoethnography—overlapping today's reality. Furthermore, is autoethnography the researcher's version of the selfie? As Dr Paul O'Connor states in *The Rise of Mesearch* in his blog:

> As I do the math, it does not seem a surprise that a calibre of research for the "Selfie Age" should take this form. I call it scholarship as a "Selfie Stick". Blogging, Facebook, Tweeting, Reality TV, and Academia.edu all bolster the argument here. [...] A final point is that perhaps me-search is a product of the new university, of austerity, and the drive for publications amidst a paucity of funding.[19]

To this extent, in this "Selfie Age", my documentary and its relation with participatory culture can be considered rather sophisticated "mesearch", where the internet and its power are growing day by day. Thus, I created my documentary four years ago; now, we have a variety of recording apps such as Snapchat or Scorp, using moving images as a core element. Four years from now, communication and its forms will become totally different; however, one

---

[16] Available at https://www.youtube.com/watch?v=ibJaqXVaOaI (Accessed: 3 June 2019)

[17] Available at https://www.youtube.com/watch?v=AFCLKa0XRlw (Accessed: 4 June 2019)

[18] A form of blog for which the medium is video; a form of web television.

[19] Available at http://everydayhybridity.tumblr.com/ (Accessed: 6 June 2019)

thing will be left the same: expression. For instance, in *Doing Qualitative Research: Circles within Circles* (2003), the writing team gives an example of an expression in its reflecting chapter for a "mesearch". They had become aware that some of the students were already thinking in terms of life-as-ethnography, or alternatively ethnography-as-life. One student, Deborah Lamb, had married during the mid-semester break, and had woven aspects of her wedding into her final paper, inviting the reader to see the research in the way that she was seeing it, i.e., through the lens of her recent nuptials. She further delved into the potential reasons why such intermingling happens:

> Some people say all research is me-research. I did not intend to have my sister's death, my mother's bout with cancer, my marriage plans or my own medical history come creeping into my field work; but like the fearfully creatures looming large as a child's imagination under bed at night, these things clamoured for a place in my study and made themselves at home. The interconnected layers of self-as-researcher and woman becoming a wife emerged in my log and began to structure the project at hand as systematically and elegantly as the tiers of the wedding cake awaiting us at Spring Break. [...] In searching for new means of accountability and trustworthiness as a researcher, I came to know more intimately my own needs. (Anzul and Margot and Teri and Diane and Ann 2003, 191)

On the other hand, in the current digital age, quick selfies are flourishing and reflecting part of one's identity. They are all around us: our selfie pictures appear on Facebook with names and surnames. We have the power to control these images and name options, where online also means anonymous. People start to explore, for example, their gender identities by altering their name. They give a voice to their concerns and questions, and experiment a bit. To put it in the context of this Selfie Age, my documentary research is, regarding changing surnames of women and my own surname investigation, not an up-to-the-minute online topic, but rather an identity crisis of the surname issue, which is connected to the state. In this respect, women's self-representation is contextualised in the communities we belong to, both online and offline. Bakhtin, in *Autobiographics: A Feminist Theory of Women's Self-representation*, comments:

> Each person's inner world and thought has its stabilised social audience that comprises the environment in which reasons, motives, values and so on are fashioned [...] Specific class and specific era are limits that the

ideal of addressee cannot go beyond. In point of fact, word is a two-sided act. It is determined equally by whose word it is and for whom it is meant. As word, it is precisely the product of the reciprocal relationship between speaker and listener, addresser and addressee. Each and every word expresses the "one" in relation to the "other". I give myself verbal shape from another's point of view ultimately from the point of view of the community to which I belong. (Gilmore 1994, 4)

The community to which I belong is composed of "writers, poets and visual artists, filmmakers, designers, finger-painters (as illustrators working with mobile devices call themselves) [and they] are using innovative forms within spaces created social media where 'creative vernaculars' (Burgess 2007, 29) and aesthetics are emerging" (Berry and Schleser 2014, 2). As stated in *Mobile Media Making in an Age of Smart Phones*, "mobile media remixes and remediates old and new media" (2014, 2) and also shapes storytelling to generate new forms. I believe it is difficult for human beings to think or to act independently from the technology and culture we live in. For example, in the research project *Me: Narcissism and its Facets as Predictors of Selfie-Posting Frequency*, Eric B. Weise (2015) strives to examine "the association between narcissism, a personality trait characterised by inflated self-views and attempts to seek attention and admiration from others, and frequency of posting selfies on social networking sites" (1).

In addition, Anne Sofia Fink (2000) discussed the researcher's important position in the research process in her article "The Role of the Researcher in the Qualitative Research Process: A Potential Barrier to Archiving Qualitative Data" as one in which the researcher is independently involved in each step taken. Thus in this Selfie Age, researching one own self is much more possible, and as such, the readers of this research need to keep that information in mind.

5.4 Life as Research

As a form of expression, television programmes, films, and moving images entertain people; however, they also do more than that. For example, Lincoln (2010) expresses the following:

Film is considered by many to be an important art form; films entertain, educate, enlighten and inspire audiences. The visual elements of cinema need no translation, giving the motion picture a universal power of communication. (132)

The cinema industry itself is a powerful source of messages, and reflects our lives. At that point, high budgets might affect the power of the communicator's message with makeup artists, visual effects, and music selection. Generally speaking, documentaries are tackled with a modest approach. For example, mine was completed on a typical student budget. Frankly, I do not think that the budget affects the message; however, one of my interviewees could not believe her eyes when I arrived with my little feathered microphone and a handheld camera. Her reaction affected my physiology in a negative way for a while; yet, I still asked all my questions. Indeed, that aura affected my mood, and automatically I did not use those scenes while in the editing process. Even that reflection can affect the output.

Furthermore, the subtle music in my documentary is by İpek Görgün, who is also my friend. Hence, the output at the end exhibits not only my reflections but also the expressions of my connections. In addition, I learned that the more you involve people in your work, the more spreadable it becomes, as the additional parties would also like to share it during or after the process, highlighting the collaborative nature of the work. It has been said that star power is another tool to increase the message's impact on the masses. Add to that, according to Rosenthal and Corner (2005), "reflexive elements in documentaries are undoubtedly a reflection of a general cultural concern with self-awareness. They are also the continuation of a tradition in visual forms of communication" (37).

After becoming aware of these so-called obstacles inside and outside of the work and self, everything came down to sharing emotions, thoughts and reactions. For example, while presenting my work at the conference Doing Autoethnography: (Re)writing Self, Other, and Society at San Angelo University on 2 March 2013, I suddenly started to cry. Without any hesitation, I continued to present my paper, because I subconsciously knew that the more vulnerable I could be, the more benefits I would receive and serve in autoethnography. I did not plan it; the emotions were spontaneous. The story that I was telling was still in my psyche, affecting me, and my tears were touching to the audience. Some even gave me handkerchiefs. During these moments, we breach the silence.

Later that night, we went to a karaoke bar, as scholars often spent some extra time together after a satisfying conference. One of my new friends from the conference gave me feedback that my work was resonating with them. Tami Spry, an autoethnography professional and keynote speaker of our conference, came with us to the karaoke bar. Spry wrote an article entitled "Call It Swing: A Jazz Blues Autoethnography", and my new academic friends were interested in music, mostly jazz. During that evening, they were singing different kinds of music, and performing to a high standard, but I refrained from participating. It occurred to me that expression with passion could be taken as a whole, not only in a karaoke bar, but also in academic work. While watching those impromptu performances, I thought that I was not going to be some random academic. If I cannot sing on the night after a conference, then what is the meaning of life?

In the book *Songwriting: Methods, Techniques and Clinical Applications for Music Therapy Clinicians, Educators and Students* (2005), edited by Felicity Baker and Tony Wigram, the role of songs has been explained as follows:

> [Songs] can assist people to reflect on their past, present or future, to make contact with unconscious thought processes, to confront difficulties within their interpersonal experiences and their interpersonal relationships, and to project their feelings into music. Songs can be used in facilitating the development or redevelopment of functional skills including physical, cognitive or communication functions. Within groups, song assist in developing group cohesiveness, encouraging social interaction and providing group support. (11)

That night, in a karaoke bar, I looked through the song list and knew most of the pop songs as a reflection of society's perception for my documentary, such as "Your Surname Stayed with You" / "Soyadın Sende Kaldı" by Ali Kanık or "You Are My Surname" / "Soyadımsın" by Murat Boz or "You Write My Surname" / "Soyadımı Sen Yaz" by Deniz Seki. These surname-related songs express how society feels. As Bruscia also states in the book *An Introduction to Music Psychotherapy*, "songs articulate our beliefs and values; [...] witness to our lives. [...] They are our musical diaries, our life-stories. They are the sounds of our personal development." (1998, 9) I did prefer to move away from surnames and their stories. Alternatively, I could have taken on some *musiki* (Ottoman traditional music) pieces, but that night I was unable to sing anything, even though I was in the US with songs in my mother tongue. The universal language of music did not work that specific night; I preferred simply to carry that experience within me.

Years passed, and in 2016 I suddenly found myself taking a jazz course conducted by Sibel Köse, a very experienced prominent jazz musician, and to this day, the story of my musical journey is still under construction. Hence, finding my way started with a camera as the instrument of expression, but even now that a microphone has taken its place, the truth remains that storytelling is storytelling. That night in that karaoke bar, I did not know that I had already instinctively used a specific form of singing method in my documentary, which included some non-verbal sounds. Afterwards I realised that me-search and me-construction have always been under way, and are an open-ended process. Within myself, there are numerous pieces of me who are talking to each other, and those selves are passing the fantastic ball to each other every day, at any moment. In conclusion, my documentary and my research process have, after a few obstacles, brought new opportunities. This in turn has created a totally new world for me, which these days is filled with joy and laughter.

5.5. Leaving Surnames Behind, Scatting without Fear

"Coincidences mean you are on the right path." (Van Booy 2014, IX)

I fully understood this sentence six years after meeting my PhD advisor, who is mostly known as a film person, a writer, and an academic. To my surprise, I discovered that she had created a book on jazz entitled *Jazz / Caz Hüznün Müziği* (1985), which sounded unbelievable to me at first. Why are some people interested in similar topics and others not? Furthermore, how do they find each other? To me, this seems magical. In this part of my research, I would like to highlight the scatting technique in jazz, and its relation with my autoethnographic research. By doing that, I aim to conclude this last chapter by opening a parallel window for my future research. Indeed, the journey of where I started and where I am headed carries a lot of clues in itself.

As I discussed before, expression is common in all forms of communication. In my case, it is just changing its clothes. To put in another way, the forms are changing but the core is the same. For example, in scat singing we come across "this buzzing moan, like humming, [...] and nonsense sounds, [serving] to fasten our attention on what is really a gap in intelligibility" (Garon 2014, 185). Hence, Tami Spry (2010) made that connection and emphasised it in the abstract as the "everyday lived methodology of swing" in her work *Call it Swing: A Jazz Blues Autoethnography.*

> This performative autoethnography utilises jazz swing as a method to further activate the critical processes in qualitative research. In reflecting on my father's 25 years as a jazz musician, I find his everyday lived methodology of swing provides an opportunity to explore the ways in which family inheritance collides with sociocultural practices of racial inequity and cultural appropriation. Autoethnographically re/inhabiting this space and sound with my father revealed a performative ethos, an empathetic epistemology of critical reflection

activated by the transgressive discipline of jazz. Specifically, this performative ethos is applied to issues of racial accountability, embodied theorising, and the ethical implications of an aesthetic / epistemic praxis in autoethnography. More broadly, I offer performative ethos as critical pedagogy assisting in living a critical life where issues of power and privilege are personally political and are written and rewritten daily with others in hope of utopia. (271)

It has been said that jazz is the democracy of music. "You have got to play. Together. You cannot play jazz alone." (Marsalis and Wigeland 2001, 167) Its roots embrace "the other", and open a lot of improvisational doors to the audience as well as to the performer. For example, James Tartaglia defines this concept in his piece entitled *Jazz-Philosophy Fusion*[20] as follows:

Not singers so much as performers, who could add something overtly conceptual to the mix, through a combination of statements and improvised acting around a theme, in addition to wordless elements: laughing, crying, sighing, screaming, and so on. (2016, 3)

These emotional effects are under-recognised in formal environments although each and every one of us is a potential political agent in a participatory culture, and has the power to speak up in our own way, creating our own protest. As in the autoethnographic research method, researchers analyse their own subjectivity and treat the self as "other" while calling attention to issues of power; similarly, jazz itself can also be considered a form of self-narrative that places the self within a social context. For example, Ingrid Monson (2009) in *Saying Something: Jazz Improvisation and Interaction* points out that by stressing music as a catalyst for community, the standard barriers to community are removed, such as location, race, class, and gender. Instead, these categories of social standing, along with everything they represent, become part of the fabric that helps create the magic of jazz performance and recording.

---

[20] "Jazz-Philosophy Fusion, his own conception, is designed to express the emotional significance of philosophical ideas, and thereby provide new inspiration to jazz music. He has explored this concept on three previous albums (*A Free Jazz Treatise*, 2002; *Dark Metaphysic*, 2008; *Kooky Steps*, 2014), but Continuum of Selves will be the first full-scale and dedicated work."
Available at http://www.jazzphilosophyfusion.com/james-tartaglia.html (Accessed: 3 June 2019)

My thinking about the community is informed, in part, by the social theory of Anthony Giddens, who suggests that social groups are constituted and reproduced by the recurrent actions of individual agents whose activities have both intended and unintended consequences. Viewed as a dynamic system through time, Giddens argues, the day-to-day activities of group members express the norms, values and expectations of a collectivity that extend beyond any one individual. The focus of cultural and social inquiry becomes the question of how the actions of social agents constitute, reproduce and transform the social entity in question. (14)

Music and conversation carry a connection. "Beginning in the 1960s both linguistics and musicologists have attempted to identify formal parallels between music and speech." (Sawyer 2005, 45) Especially in jam sessions, jazz musicians improvise together in impromptu gatherings. The American Heritage Dictionary[21] defines the jam session as both a type of jazz performance and also as an impromptu or highly informal discussion. When you sit at a bountiful table in the evening or on a sunny Sunday morning at breakfast, while descanting upon a subject—for instance, a film for which everyone has an enthusiastic opinion—it has been said that this is the feeling of jazz.

Everyone is participating in the dialogue, with the tools and instruments that are sentences; they are playing a sort of game. It resembles the concept of spreadable media, in which each of us shapes the content. So much so that, if the "auto" is "scatting" then the "ethno" would be "the ensemble" (auto + ethno = scat singing + ensemble). R. Keith Sawyer also states the following:

Jamming refers to the collective activity of group creating together. Group creativity is found not only in music; it is essential in many problem-solving groups, such as brainstorming session at a high-technology company, a group of teachers collaborating to develop new curriculum, or a family working to resolve a financial crisis. In group performance, the creativity of performance depends on an intangible chemistry between the members of the group. In jazz, for example no musician can determine the flow of the performance: It emerges out of the musical conversation, a give-and-take as performers propose new

---

[21] Available at https://ahdictionary.com/word/search.html?q=jam+session (Accessed: 3 June 2019)

ideas, respond to other's ideas, and elaborate or modify those ideas as the performance moves forward. (Berliner 2009, 47)

My filmmaking experience spread the seeds, gave birth to this research and created a researcher—me, in this case. Inevitably my documentary and research reflect my personal his-story, in which inner communication drives me forward. Whenever I am investigating my inner world or talking to myself, that process becomes a bigger project later on. We need a dialogue rather than a monologue, and to do more scat singing in jazz, similar to Virginia Woolf's well-known stream of consciousness technique in literature. I dug deeper and, after all my research on surname, feminism and filmmaking, I moved onto a parallel path, discovering something that had been like an elephant in the room for years. I am now joining the flow of a new river, and putting jazz expression in the centre. Thus, I am busy discovering my new, strong women—not new for the world, but for me. These include Nina Simone and her people's struggle in "Ain't Got No, I've Got Life", or Billie Holiday in "Strange Fruit", describing the murder of black people who were hanged from trees, or Ella Fitzgerald and her improvisational performance of "Air Mail Special". Musical communication has so much in common with everyday social life. There is no director in jazz, and no score for musicians to scat from. I also understand that from this expression comes the freedom of unpredictability, the joy of plurality, and the politics of dialogue. Finally, I met the little girl in me, who is singing all the time. As I arrive at the end of this journey, I remember that singing jazz tunes is only a metaphor, whereas in our lives, as female agents, we all have the power to discover our deconstructive singing-like experiences in families, schools, or institutions, if we look inward and follow our own paths rather than the pre-constructed courses presented to us.

In order to scat without fear at the end, I came to the conclusion that I had to walk all these "surname" paths beforehand. When I was nearing the end of this chapter, I remember from Özden Melis Uluğ's article (2015) "My Name is My Identity and Must not be Lost: a Critical Perspective on the Relationship Between Hegemonic Masculinity and Article 187 of the Civil Code"[22], which plays an important role "in reproducing hegemonic masculinity by providing the possibility of reconstructing the paternalistic system through men" (1) that she made a statement regarding "a woman who has built a career before her marriage has to rebuild her career after marriage with a different surname,

---

[22] Here is the original name: Özden Melis Uluğ, "Soyadım Kimliğimdir, Evlenince Kaybolmamalıdır": Hegemonik Erkeklik ile Medeni Kanun'un 187. Maddesi Arasındaki İlişkiye Eleştirel Bir Bakış" Fe Dergi 7, no. 2 (2015), 48-58.

constituting a disadvantage for women in terms of gender equality" (1). Sırma Oya Tekvar, another scholar "who opened a trial to 're-gain her identity and register that had changed upon her marriage'. The court rejected her claim in the first hearing of the case. Tekvar described the decision as an 'extrajudicial execution' [and] she commented, 'Women have to realise that the change of the women's surname with marriage is an open indicator of discrimination."[23] I agreed with her, and we got together for my documentary; however, I could not complete the process for technical reasons. Tekvar's lawyer Alev Yıldız[24] also helped us on the day I met with Tekvar by sharing her unique experience on the surname cases. Incidentally, some media hassled her about the title of "Beautiful Oya's Surname Suffering" / "Güzel Oya'nın Soyadı Çilesi", and she criticised this response in one of her interviews:

> They would like to see me only in the context of beauty. A beautiful and moody woman... she has no other issues other than her surname! The news item was copy-pasted; however, this title of "Beautiful Oya's Surname Suffering" explained everything. Sometimes the surname issue appears on the agenda with the emphasis on women's beauty.

---

[23] "Tekvar married Prof. Haluk Geray, Dean of the Ankara University Faculty of Communications, on 17 October 2009. Without her consent she was forced to adopt her husband's surname Geray together with her maiden name. Haluk Geray applied to adopt both his own and his wife's name after marriage, but this request was dismissed by the Turkish Civil Court, Tekvar said. The first hearing was held on 16 December before the Ankara 2nd Family Court. Tekvar's request was rejected for the following reasons: Article 187 of the Turkish Civil Code (Law No. 4721) stipulates that 'married women shall bear their husband's name. However, they can make a written declaration to the Registrar of Births, Marriages and Deaths on signing the marriage deed or at the Registry of Births, Marriages and Deaths after the marriage, if they wish to keep their maiden name in front of their surname. Women who previously carried two surnames can only benefit from this law for one name.' Applying Article 187 of the Civil Code, women are obliged to bear their husband's name, and at the same time this is being evaluated as a right granted to women. As a matter of fact, no woman can object to bearing her husband's name. As long as she is married, the woman is obliged to bear her husband's name and she cannot change her surname if the marriage ends." Available at http://bianet.org/ bianet/english/126665-a-womans-right-and-obligation-to-carry-her-husbands-name (Accessed: 5 June 2019)

[24] "Alev Yıldız also represented Assoc. Prof. Ebru Voyvoda from the Middle East Technical University in a similar case tried at the ECHR. This was the first trial of its kind that was won, a precedent for the Turkish judiciary." Available at http://bianet.org/bianet/ english/126665-a-womans-right-and-obligation-to-carry-her-husbands-name (Accessed: 4 June 2019)

Because with a lot of serious issues going on, the implication is that this is an "unimportant" one.[25] (translated by me)

Recently I contacted Yıldız to ask for advice. As I made a statement in the surname chapter that the problem is not changing at all in Turkey, one of my instructors shared a news article[26] with me that reported a real possibility of change in the new law code. In the news, it has been asserted that HDP İstanbul's representative in the Grand National Assembly of Turkey, feminist lawyer Filiz Kerestecioğlu, put forward a motion regarding women's rights to use their original surnames. When I enquired about the issue with Alev Yıldız, she informed me that no laws had changed; however, that the issue is still being dealt with, and she sent me the relevant documents. Furthermore, I have communicated with Kerestecioglu's assistant, and got the impression that nothing at all is changing or even being taken seriously; however, apart from that, Kerestecioğlu's attempt is obviously giving hope to many of us. Gülşah Kaya, her assistant, shared the following with me via email with permission to mention it in my research:

Kerestecioğlu gave the notice of motion on 15 July 2015. It was just after the 7 June elections. So, it fell through the cracks. There was not even any discussion about it... However, after the 1 November elections, an extensive petition was presented. [...] As far as I know, Kerestecioğlu met with the Ministry of Family and Social Policy, and no results again. What is funny is that recently (13-14 April 2016) the Ministry of Family and Social Policy discussed harassment, abuse, violence; however the surname issue was not on the agenda. On the contrary, they said that "divorced women do not take children around to see their ex-husbands anyway, so this is unacceptable, as alieni juris arbitration would have to be overhauled." So, there is no sign that there is going to be any change. (translated by me) (2016, 1)

---

[25] Available at https://bianet.org/bianet/print/146561-yok-anasinin-soyadi (Accessed: 20 June 2019)

[26] Available at http://www.cumhuriyet.com.tr/haber/turkiye/323261/Kadinin_soyadi_ hakki_icin_kanun_teklifi_verildi. html (Accessed: 20 June 2019)

Although representation of the issue is quite hopeless in Parliament[27], a lot of women are stressing, struggling, and seriously working on this issue. For instance, Sultan Komut wrote (2012) in the article "Do Women Have a Right to Keep Their Surname? Stances of Women Living in İstanbul on Their Right to Use Their Own Surname"[28] that "giving up surname means giving up identity and when someone loses her identity, gradually she gives up everything" (1). Moreover, I remember Meral Tamer's writing[29] in which she emphasises an example of a young man who would like to stay in a hotel room with his divorced mother, but feels like a gigolo because of their different surnames and the related societal judgement. Hence, it is not only women who are affected by this issue, but also some men. CANAN[30], a contemporary feminist artist, is another example of one who rejects paternal and marital surnames; indeed, she rejects the entire concept of surnames, and publishes her work with her first name only in capital letters. I am glad that there are many strong role models we had, have, and will have.

These days I find myself thinking back to an old ritual: in high school, if we girls had crushes on some of the boys, we would daydream that one day we would become their respective wives. Furthermore, we daydreamed about

---

[27] I see the similarities between the surname change of minorities during the construction of the nation-state and the surname changes of the women in the family system. For example, in the "Surname Law of 1934 that forbids Turkish citizens from adopting foreign last names in a lawsuit filed by Favlus Ay, a Turkish citizen of Syriac descent, who wanted to change his name to Paulus Bartuma. Ay first appealed to a court in Midyat, a district in the southeastern province of Mardin, but the suit was then sent to the Constitutional Court which rejected the appeal by a very small margin, with eight judges ruling against the law and nine in favour. [...] 'Politicians say the important thing is the bond of citizenship, whereas the laws are forcing everyone to become a Turk. It is not only Turks who live in Turkey; this is an extremely chauvinistic attitude' Ahmet Fazıl Tamer, a lawyer working for the Human Rights Association, or the IHD, told the *Daily News* by phone. [...] 'An individual bears no such responsibility in terms of explaining or proving anything. A person should be able to adopt any first and last name of their choice in a democratic system' Tamer said." Available at http://www.hurriyetdailynews.com/default.aspx? pageid=438&n=turkey8217s-syriacs-demanding-right-to-own-names-2011-07-13 (Accessed: 3 June 2019)

[28] Komut, Sultan. "(K)Adının Soyadı Hakkı Var Mı?: İstanbul'da Yasayan Kadınların Kendi Soyadlarını Kullanma Hakkı Konusundaki Tutumları." Sosyal ve Beşeri Bilimler Dergisi 4.2: 2012.

[29] Available at http://www.milliyet.com.tr/annesiyle-soyadi-farkli-oldugu-icin-jigolo-sanmislar-/ekonomi/ekonomiyazardetay/19.02.2012/1505090/default.htm (Accessed: 5 June 2019)

[30] Available at http://www.artfulliving.com.tr/sanat/kadin-sanatci-tanimi-beni-rahatsiz-ediyor-i-4908 (Accessed: 7 June 2019)

having these boys' surnames by changing ours temporarily, as a game. As time passed, I came to understand that my surname was not a game, but rather my identity. The important matter nowadays for me is to look forward, and I realise that being aware of this surname issue, in many aspects, and walking the path rather than ignoring it, prompted me to act, which in turn prepared me to sing freely with all those fighters now. Thus, it started with pressure via my surname, through to my very personal identity. At first, I rolled with the punches, and later turned the oppression into jazz expression, which conversely took me to a free and collaborative place.

Conclusion

This practice-led documentary-research, which gave me the opportunity to gain both academic and inner vision, pushed forward the desire to understand my own decisions and acts as an emerging researcher and woman, to be carried through in an independent world. Through this process, I figured out the aim of the scientific research and came to answer critical questions around it. The discoveries in this creative research propose to look deeply into the researcher herself, where as a woman I was repeatedly oppressed. I was initially against external discourses where my subjectivity and experience-based approach would be evaluated as vulnerable and off-topic, as the socially-constructed society more readily accepts the white, masculine, rich, and Western.

In a system where my identity, that is to say my surname, was taken from me when I got married, and where the state and families supported it, I was simply a woman in a personal space at home, which was upsetting. When I did not accept the given role, did not use that given marriage surname, and reacted against it, I became curious about other women's decisions and made a documentary. In a socially-constructed environment, I promoted individual power, grounded in politics where I shared and spread my act via old and new media as a member of this participatory culture. My performativity collided with the community that I belong to and created a collaborative meaning.

In this Selfie Age we live in, speaking up to the masses is easy. Hence I used social media to spread my message: I am not going to change my surname. It was a visual sign, a cultural code, with my feelings in between—a decision in the making. Although it was only about self-expression in the beginning, it grew like a dandelion and gave its seeds. After spreading that message, I turned my attention to jazz pedagogy. As a human being, I found my way; however, if I had not walked this PhD path for the last six years, I am not sure if I would now be able to mimic musical instruments and sing improvisationally. During this research, I figured out that creativity is a collaborative process where most creative projects flow in improvisation. I did this collaborative documentary, wrote this practice-led research, and spread the process in flow because I wanted to "be the change I would like to see in this world". The difference in my story, in which I got divorced and started to sing jazz, is worth mentioning because this change started with the rejection of the systematic structure of using a husband's surname. During this process, I found out that I was singing more skilfully when I was six, when I believe the system (e.g., school, family, and state) kept me in the dark.

I aimed to use insights and knowledge gained through this PhD, and I settled an account with my story and faced its alienation by the help of autoethnography. I learned that our lives empower our research, and our research empowers our lives where human beings (auto)-connect with world they live in (ethno), and attaining knowledge is possible by starting with our own stories, which are not different from others' stories. I understood that human beings are the reasons for a life story; however, systematically, there is praise when we diverge from ourselves. As a researcher in this Selfie Age, I conducted an autoethnographical documentary "investigation into female subjectivity" (Sexton Finck 2009, 1), and my research argues that it would be courageous for researchers to protest their domestic status and deconstruct the patriarch.

Introducing a woman as the centre of a research was an attempt to establish that future research would benefit from women's knowledge. As an example, I broke the connection and stopped listening to my husband and my father and their representational status in life, i.e., "the dos and don'ts" of the patriarchy. I gained inner power, boosted by an understanding of the "performativity"[1] of our identities. As these social structures created an illusion with its norms, codes, and contracts, I aimed to act, do, be, write, shoot a documentary, divorce, sing jazz, and earn a PhD so as to survive within those structures, where we do have endless options to act and participate in our daily lives. Conventions and ideologies of this socially-constructed world make themselves real if we do not react. This book is a reaction, as is my documentary. The sense of subjectivity is the source of our actions and is a new construction. I learned that even the way we carry our names is designed to support oppressive mechanisms and social conventions.

This research offered me an opportunity to break free from society's unrealistic approaches to femininity. I have presented examples that carry endless determinants to define self. One's sur(name) must be her / his own decision. Men are oppressing woman, but the established conventions and ideologies are oppressing them as well. Female passivity is a construction, and feminism gave us the power to speak up so that acting and spreading acts is possible at any time. Also, in academia—another system— one can study him / herself, which can be considered a powerful act, challenging the norms. As "writing vulnerably, evocatively and ethically" (Ellis 2004, 119) is the core

---

[1] Butler, Judith. *"Performative Agency."*Journal of Cultural Economy 3, no. 2 (2010): 147-161.

element of autoethnography—instead of dealing with hypotheses—the emphasis is a process of slice-of-life discovery (Ellis 2004, 10) and vivid descriptions. (Ellis 2004, 60) Hopefully, this research will represent a significant output for academia, as Turkish resources are limited to the extent that only a few major books on the subject have been published in Turkey: *Kadının Soyadı / Women's Surnames* by Nazan Moroğlu and *Kadının Soyadı ve Buna Bağlı Olarak Çocuğun Soyadı / Women's Surnames and Corresponding Children's Surnames* by Yıldız Abik. Both writers are lawyers; as a result of this, both books are written from a forensic point of view, and both lack personal stories. That is to say, it is important to produce and to share knowledge using autoethnography, to tell our own stories. I also found out that Harika Esra Oskay Malicki's PhD thesis (2014) *Home-work: A Study of Home at the Threshold of Autoethnography and Art Practice* is the only source from Turkish academia that involves autoethnography in the title, which demonstrates the lack of samples in the field in which I hope to contribute.

My view is that shifting women's position in society does not start from changing the law, but rather traditional patriarchal mechanisms. It starts with individuals simply saying no to changing their surnames, or to their oppressive fathers, husbands, or bosses—whatever the authority is. It also starts with offering uncanny academic methods for PhD research such as autoethnography, along with continuity in performance-based acts, deconstructing "given" methods, learning jazz, regaining a certain freedom in singing, and spreading the message to a community. By doing that, I offer that we are becoming myopic to mainstream ideologies and our open-endedness will be influenced, where at that moment the discipline is not important: it can be an autoethnographical documentary, an unusual methodology, a theory around the margins like feminism, or a participatory culture that creates collaborative interrogation so as to delve into one's "self" in the presence of "other" people to obtain collective experiences and gain knowledge. The goal is to evolve and shift the acceptance of fluctuating self as a social subject in those auto+ethno (method), scat+ensemble (jazz), personal+political (self), individual+collaborative (participatory culture), and me+you (documentary) spheres, in which we tell stories that reflect our own experiences as a critical self-reflexive discourse, while adding our emotions in detail and focusing on ourselves as researchers and filmmakers. At that point, the "private" inevitably becomes "public", and it is a process that bridges the autobiographical, personal to cultural, social, and political (Ellis 2004). And, I believe that eventually—given the potential of spreadability and circulation of meaning—my story became (y)ours.

Bibliography

Abik, Yıldız. *Kadının Soyadı ve Buna Bağlı Olarak Çocuğun Soyadı.* Seçkin, 2005.

Adams, Tony E., and Stacy Holman Jones. *"Telling Stories: Reflexivity, Queer Theory, and Autoethnography."* Cultural Studies ↔ Critical Methodologies 11, no. 2, April 2011: 108-116.

Allen, Daniel C. *"Learning Autoethnography: A Review of Autoethnography: Understanding Qualitative Research."* The Qualitative Report 20.2, 2015: 33-35.

Almack, Kathryn. *"What's in a Name? The Significance of the Choice of Surnames Given to Children Born within Lesbian-Parent Families."* Sexualities 8, no. 2, 2005: 239-254.

Altınay, Ayşe Gül, and Yeşim Arat. *Violence Against Women in Turkey: a Nationwide Survey.* Punto, 2009.

Angelou, Maya. *I Know Why the Caged Bird Sings.* Bantam, 1997.

Anzul, Margaret, Margot Ely, Teri Freidman, Diane Garner, and Ann McCormack-Steinmetz. *Doing Qualitative Research: Circles within Circles.* Routledge, 2003.

Arat, Yeşim. *"Women's Movement of the 1980s in Turkey: Radical Outcome of Liberal Kemalism?" Reconstructing gender in the Middle East: Tradition, Identity, and Power.* Columbia University Press, 1994.

Bachmann, Ingeborg. *The Book of Franza and Requiem for Fanny Goldmann.* Northwestern University Press, 2010.

Baker, Felicity, and Tony Wigram. *Songwriting: Methods, Techniques and Clinical Applications for Music Therapy Clinicians, Educators and Students.* Jessica Kingsley Publishers, 2005.

Barclay, Katie. *What's in a Name? Or Leaving Your Patrilineage Behind.* Women's History Network. May 23, 2010.
https://womenshistorynetwork.org/whats-in-a-name-or-leaving-your-patrilineage-behind/ [Accessed: 4 January 2020]

Barlas, Asma. *Believing Women in İslam: Unreading Patriarchal Interpretations of the Qur'an.* University of Texas Press, 2009.

Barthes, Roland. *"The Death of the Author."* Contributions in Philosophy 83, 2001: Ubu Web papers.

Bates, Charlotte. *Video Methods: Social Science Research in Motion.* Vol. 10. Routledge, 2014.

Baudrillard, Jean, and G. Thompson. *The Evil Demon of Images and the Precession of Simulacra. Postmodernism: A reader.* Columbia University Press, 1993.

Bayles, David, and Ted Orland. *Art and Fear: Observations on the Perils (and rewards) of Artmaking.* Image Continuum Press, 2001.

Bayraktar, Özlem. *Ekranda Bir Kadın Olarak Kendine Yer Açmak*. Web. 10 July 2016. https://www.academia.edu/4682609/Ekranda_Bir_Kad%C4%B1n_Olarak_K endine_Yer_A%C3%A7mak [Accessed: 21 July 2006]

Beauvoir, Simone de. *The Second Sex*. Trans. Constance Borde and Sheila Malovany-Chevallier. Random House: Alfred A. Knopf, (2009) [1949].

Behar, Ruth. *The Vulnerable Observer: Anthropology That Breaks Your Heart*. Beacon Press, 2014.

Berktay, Fatmagül. *Women and Religion*. Black Rose Books Limited, 1998.

Berktay, Fatmagül. *Tarihin Cinsiyeti*. Metis, 2003.

Berliner, Paul F. *Thinking in Jazz: The Infinite Art of Improvisation*. University of Chicago Press, 2009.

Berry, Marsha, and Max Schleser, eds. *Mobile Media Making in an Age of Smartphones*. Palgrave Macmillan, 2014.

Bolter, Jay David, and Remediation Grusin. *"Understanding New Media."* MIT Press, 1999.

Boylorn, Robin M., and Mark P. Orbe, eds. *Critical Autoethnography: Intersecting Cultural Identities in Everyday Life*. Vol. 13. Left Coast Press, 2013.

Bruno, Giuliana. *Atlas of Emotion: Journeys in Art, Architecture, and Film*. Verso, 2002.

Bruno, Giuliana. *"Passages Through Time and Space: In Memory of Chantal Akerman."* October, 2016: 162-167.

Bruno, Giuliana. *"Projection: On Chantal Akerman's Screens, from Cinema to the Art Gallery."* Senses of Cinema 7, 2015.

Bruscia, K. E. (1998). *An Introduction to Music Psychotherapy*. In K. Bruscia (Ed.), The Dynamics of Music Psychotherapy, pp. 1–15. Gilsum NH: Barcelona Publishers.

Butler, Judith. *"Performative Agency."* Journal of Cultural Economy 3, no. 2, 2010: 147-161.

Bysiewicz, Shirley Raissi, and Gloria Jeanne Stillson MacDonnell. *"Married Women's Surnames."* Conn. L. Rev. 5, 1972: 598.

Chang, Heewon. *Autoethnography as Method*. Developing Qualitative Inquiry, v. 1. Walnut Creek, Calif: Left Coast Press, 2008.

Chodorow, Nancy J. *The Power of Feelings: Personal Meaning in Psychoanalysis, Gender, and Culture*. New Haven, Conn. London: Yale University Press, 1999.

Çiçekoğlu, Feride. *Caz Hüznün Müziği*. Kalem Yayıncılık, 1985.

Cixous, Hélène, Keith Cohen, and Paula Cohen. *"The Laugh of the Medusa."* Signs: Journal of Women in Culture and Society 1, no. 4, July 1976: 875-893.

Cohan, Steven, and Ina Rae Hark, eds. *Screening the Male: Exploring Masculinities in the Hollywood Cinema*. Routledge, 2012.

Coulombeau, Sophie. *"Why Should Women Change Their Names on Getting Married?"* BBC News Websites. 1 Nov. 2014. [Accessed: 21 July 2016]

Curthoys, Jean. *Feminist Amnesia: The Wake of Women's Liberation.* Routledge, 2003.

Davies, Hayley. *"Sharing Surnames: Children, Family and Kinship."* Sociology 45, No. 4, 2011: 554-569.

Denzin, Norman K. *Interpretive Ethnography.* Second Edition, Volume 17. United States: Sage, 2014.

Derrida, Jacques. *"The Truth in Painting, trans. Geoff Bennington and Ian McLeod."* Chicago: University of Chicago Press 26, 1987: 373.

Diamond, Elin. *Unmaking Mimesis: Essays on Feminism and Theatre.* Routledge, 2003.

Doctorow, Cory. *"Think Like a Dandelion."* Locus Magazine, online: http://www. locusmag. com/Features/2008/05/cory-doctorow-think-like-dandelion.html. [Accessed: 11 April 2016]

Eco, Umberto, and Stefan Collini. *Interpretation and Overinterpretation.* Cambridge University Press, 1992.

Eco, Umberto. *The Role of the Reader: Explorations in the Semiotics of Texts.* Vol. 318. Indiana University Press, 1984.

Edelman, Lee. *No Future: Queer Theory and the Death Drive.* Duke University Press, 2004.

Ellis, Carolyn S., and Arthur Bochner. *"Autoethnography, Personal Narrative, Reflexivity: Researcher as Subject."* 2000, The Handbook of Qualitative Research: 733-768. London: Sage.

Ellis, Carolyn, Tony E. Adams, and Arthur P. Bochner. *"Autoethnography: an Overview."* Historical Social Research/Historische Sozialforschung, 2011: 273-290.

Ellis, Carolyn. *The Ethnographic I: A Methodological Novel about Autoethnography.* Ethnographic Alternatives Book Series, v. 13. Walnut Creek, CA: AltaMira Press, 2004.

Ellis, Carolyn. *"Sociological Introspection and Emotional Experience."* Symbolic Interaction 14, no. 1, 1991: 23-50.

Engels, Friedrich, and Lewis Henry Morgan. *The Origin of the Family, Private Property and the State.* Moscow: Foreign Languages Publishing House, 1978.

Eryaman, Mustafa Yunus. *"From Whirling to Trembling: A Montage of Dervishes' Performative Inquiries."* Qualitative Inquiry 18, no. 1, 2012: 55-62.

Etaugh, Claire E., Judith S. Bridges, Myra Cummings-Hill, and Joseph Cohen. *"'Names Can Never Hurt Me?' The Effects of Surname Use on Perceptions of Married Women."* Psychology of Women Quarterly 23, no. 4, 1999: 819-823.

Etherington, Kim. *Becoming a Reflexive Researcher: Using Our Selves in Research.* Jessica Kingsley Publishers, 2004.

Fink, Anne Sofia. *"The Role of the Researcher in the Qualitative Research Process. A Potential Barrier to Archiving Qualitative Data."* In Forum Qualitative Sozialforschung/Forum: Qualitative Social Research, Vol. 1, No. 3. 2000.

Foucault, Michel. *Technologies of the Self: a Seminar with Michel Foucault.* University of Massachusetts Press, 1988.

Foucault, Michel. *Power/Knowledge: Selected Interviews and Other Writings,* 1972-1977. Pantheon, 1980.

Freud, Sigmund, Joyce Crick, and Sigmund Freud. *The Joke and Its Relation to the Unconscious.* Penguin Classics. London ; New York, N.Y: Penguin, 2002.

Friedman, Lawrence Meir, and Lawrence M. Friedman. *The Human Rights Culture: A Study in History and Context.* Quid Pro Books, 2011.

Garon, Paul, and Beth Garon. *Woman with Guitar: Memphis Minnie's Blues.* City Lights Books, 2014.

Gebhardt, Nicholas, Nichole Rustin-Paschal, and Tony Whyton, eds. *The Routledge Companion to Jazz Studies.* Routledge, 2018.

Geertz, Clifford. *The Interpretation of Cultures: Selected Essays.* Vol. 5019. New York: Basic Books, 1973.

Gilmore, Leigh. *Autobiographics: a Feminist Theory of Women's Self-Representation.* Cornell University Press, 1994.

Goffman, Erving. *"The Presentation of Self in Everyday Life. 1959."* Garden City, NY, 2002.

Griffith, Elisabeth. *In Her Own Right: The life of Elizabeth Cady Stanton.* Oxford University Press, 1984.

Hamilton, Mary Agnes. *"Women in Politics."* The Political Quarterly 3, no. 2, 1932: 226-244.

Haneke, Michael. *The Paris Review Sites: Interviews, The Art of Screenwriting.* No. 5, Interviewed by Luisa Zielinski, 2014. [Accessed: 21 July 2016]

Hanisch, Carol. *"The Personal Is Political."* Notes from the Second Year: Women's Liberation (1970): New York Radical Feminism, 76-78.

Harding, Thomas, and Anita Roddick. *The Video Activist Handbook.* London: Pluto Press, 2001.

Harris-Lacewell, Melissa Victoria. *Barbershops, Bibles, and BET: Everyday Talk and Black Political Thought.* Princeton University Press, 2010.

Heider, Karl G. *"What Do People Do? Dani Auto-ethnography."* Journal of Anthropological Research, 1975: 3-17.

Henderson, Jennifer Jacobs, and Aaron Delwiche. *"Introduction: What Is Participatory Culture?."* In The Participatory Cultures Handbook, pp. 21-27. Routledge, 2012.

Holman Jones, Stacy, and Tony E. Adams. *"Autoethnography Is a Queer Method."* Queer Methods and Methodologies, 2010: 195-214.

hooks, bell. *Feminist Theory: From Margin to Center.* 2. ed. London: Pluto Press, 2000.

Jenkins, Henry, Sam Ford, and Joshua Green. *Spreadable Media: Creating Value and Meaning in a Networked Culture.* NYU press, 2013.

Jenkins, Henry, et al. *Confronting the Challenges of Participatory Culture: Media Education for the 21st Century.* Mit Press, 2009.

Jule, Allyson. *A Beginner's Guide to Language and Gender.* Multilingual Matters, 2008.

Jupp, Victor, and Sage Publications, eds. *The Sage Dictionary of Social Research Methods*. London; Thousand Oaks, Calif: SAGE Publications, 2006.

Klages, Mary. *Literary Theory: A Guide for the Perplexed*. A&C Black, 2006.

Komut, Sultan. *"(K)Adının Soyadı Hakkı Var Mı?: İstanbul'da Yasayan Kadınların Kendi Soyadlarını Kullanma Hakkı Konusundaki Tutumları."* Sosyal ve Beşeri Bilimler Dergisi 4.2: 2012.

Lamber, Julia C. *"A Married Woman's Surname: Is Custom Law."* Wash. ULQ, 1973: 779.

Langlois, Ganaele. *"Participatory Culture and the New Governance of Communication the Paradox of Participatory Media."* Television and New Media 14.2, 2013: 91-105.

Lazarre, Jane. *Beyond the Whiteness of Whiteness: Memoir of a White Mother of Black Sons*. Duke University Press, 1996.

Leavy, Patricia. *"A Review of Rufus Stone: The Promise of Arts-Based Research."* The Qualitative Report 17, no. 37, 2012: 1-3.

Leavy, Patricia. *Method Meets Art: Arts-based Research Practice*. Guilford Publications, 2015.

Lebow, Alisa, ed. *The Cinema of Me: The Self and Subjectivity in First Person Documentary*. London; New York: Wallflower Press, 2012.

Lincoln, MM. *Fundamentals of Communication Skills*. Mangalam Publishers, 2010.

Monson, Ingrid. *Saying Something: Jazz Improvisation and Interaction*. University of Chicago Press, 2009.

MacDougall, David. *"Anthropological Filmmaking: an Empirical Art."* The Sage Handbook of Visual Research Methods, 2011: 99-113.

MacDougall, Priscilla Ruth. *"Married Women's Common Law Right to Their Own Surnames."* Women's Rts. L. Rep. 1, 1971: 2.

Madden, Raymond. *Being Ethnographic: A Guide to the Theory and Practice of Ethnography*. Sage, 2010.

Malkani, Bharat. "Voices of the Condemned: A Comparative Study of the Testimonies of Death Row Exonerees and Slave Narratives." *Law, Culture and the Humanities*: Sage Publications, 2014.

Moroğlu, Nazan. *Kadının Soyadı*. Beta Yayını, İstanbul, 1999.

Mossman, Mary Jane. *"Telling the Stories of Women in Law."* Canadian Journal of Women and the Law 26, no. 2, 2014: 451-463.

Mungan, Murathan. *Yüksek Topuklar*. Metis Yayınları, 2002.

Muhammad, Bilal R. *The African American Odyssey*. AuthorHouse, 2011.

Mulvey, Laura. *"Visual Pleasure and Narrative Cinema."* In Visual and Other Pleasures, pp. 14-26. Palgrave Macmillan, London, 1989.

Myers, Mitzi. *"Mary Wollstonecraft Godwin Shelley: the Female Author Between Public and Private Spheres."* Mary Shelley in Her Times, 2003: 160-172.

Myrdal, Gunnar. *The Political Element in the Development of Economic Theory*, trans. by Paul Streeten. London: Routledge & Kegan Paul, Ltd, 1953.

Ngunjiri, Faith Wambura, Kathy-Ann C. Hernandez, and Heewon Chang. *"Living Autoethnography: Connecting Life and Research."* Journal of research practice 6, no. 1, 2010: 1.

Nichols, Bill. *Representing Reality: Issues and Concepts in Documentary*. Vol. 681. Indiana University Press, 1991.

Nimkulrat, Nithikul. *"The Role of Documentation in Practice-led Research."* Journal of Research Practice 3.1, 2007, ArticleM6.

Nunn, Nathan. *The Long-Term Effects of Africa's Slave Trades*. No. w13367. National Bureau of Economic Research, 2007.

Oskay Malicki, Harika Esra. *"Home-work: A Study of Home at the Threshold of Autoethnography and Art Practice."* University of Edinburgh, PhD Thesis, 2014.

Öymen, Şadan Maraş. *Orada Kadınlar Var Mı?* Doğan Egmont Yayıncılık, 2016.

Parks, Rosa, and James Haskins. *I Am Rosa Parks*. Dial Books for Young Readers, 1997.

Parman, Talat. *"Merhaba Bebek, Merhaba Aile." Bireyin Dogumu ve Adlandırma.* Psikanaliz Yazıları Baharlık Kitap Dizisi 15, 2007: 43-56.

Phifer, Nan. *Memoirs of the Soul: A Writing Guide*. Ingot Press, 2011.

Pink, Sarah. *Doing Visual Ethnography*. Sage Publications, 2013.

Prasad, Anshuman. *"The Gaze of the Other: Postcolonial Theory and Organizational Analysis."* In Postcolonial Theory and Organizational Analysis: a Critical Engagement, pp. 3-43. Palgrave Macmillan, New York, 2003.

Reed Danahay, Deborah. *Auto/ethnography*. New York: Berg, 1997.

Ronai, Carol R. *"My Mother Is Mentally Retarded."* Composing Ethnography: Alternative forms of qualitative writing 1, 1996: 109-131.

Rosenthal, Alan, and John Corner. *New Challenges for Documentary*. Manchester University Press, 2005.

Rosenthal, Gabriele. *Reconstruction of Life Stories: Principles of Selection in Generating Stories for Narrative Biographical Interviews*. The Narrative Study of Lives. 1993, 1 (1), 59-91.

Ruby, Jay. *Picturing Culture: Explorations of Film and Anthropology*. University of Chicago Press, 2000.

Ruby, Jay. *"The Ethics of Imagemaking: or, "They're Going to Put Me in the Movies. They're Going to Make a Big Star Out of Me"* New Challenges for Documentary, 2005: 209-219.

Saltz, Jerry. *"Art at Arm's Length: A History of the Selfie." New York Magazine* 47.2, 2014: 71-75.

Sapsford, Roger, and Victor Jupp, eds. *Data Collection and Analysis*. Sage Publications, 2006.

Sawyer, R. Keith. *"Music and Conversation."* Musical Communication, 2005: Oxford Index, 45-60.

Schreiber, Flora Rheta. *"Sybil: The Classic True Story of a Woman Possessed by Sixteen Different Personalities."* New York: Warner Books, 1973.

Sexton Finck, Larissa Claire. *"Be(com)ing Reel Independent Woman: an Autoethnographic Journey through Female Subjectivity and Agency in Contemporary Cinema with Particular Reference to Independent Scriptwriting Practice."* PhD diss., Murdoch University, 2009.

Sirman, Nükhet. *"Feminism in Turkey: A Short History."* New Perspectives on Turkey 3, 1989: New Perspectives on Turkey, 1-34.

Slater, Maya. *The Craft of LaFontaine*. Bloomsbury Publishing, 2001.

Smith, Sidonie, and Julia Watson. "Life Narrative: Definitions and Distinctions." *Reading Autobiography: A Guide for Interpreting Life Narratives*. University of Minnesota Press. 2010: 1-21.

Spence, Donald P. *"Narrative Truth and Theoretical Truth."* The Psychoanalytic Quarterly 51, no. 1, 1982: 43-69.

Spry, Tami. *"Call It Swing: A Jazz Blues Autoethnography."* Cultural Studies ↔ Critical Methodologies. 10, No. 4, August 2010: 271–82.

Spry, Tami. *"Performing Autoethnography: An Embodied Methodological Praxis."* Qualitative inquiry 7, no. 6, 2001: 706-732.

Tartaglia, James. P. F. *"Jazz-Philosophy Fusion."* Performance Philosophy 2, no. 1, 2016: 1-16.

Taylor, Jacqueline. *"On Being an Exemplary Lesbian: My Life as a Role Model."* Text and Performance Quarterly 20.1, 2000: 58-73.

Tekeli, Şirin. *Women in Modern Turkish Society: a Reader.* Zed Books, 1995.

Thwaites, Rachel. *"The Making of Selfhood: Naming Decisions on Marriage."* Families, Relationships and Societies 2, no. 3, 2013: 425-439.

Tillmann-Healy, Lisa M. *"A Secret Life in the Culture of Thinness."* Composing Ethnography: Alternative forms of qualitative writing, 1996: 76-108.

Tompkins, Jane P. *A Life in School: What the Teacher Learned.* Basic Books, 1996.

Twenge, Jean M. *"'Mrs His Name': Women's Preferences For Married Names."* Psychology of Women Quarterly 21, no. 3, September 1997: 417-429.

Uluğ, Özden Melis. *"Soyadım Kimliğimdir, Evlenince Kaybolmamalıdır": Hegemonik Erkeklik ile Medeni Kanun'un 187. Maddesi Arasındaki İlişkiye Eleştirel Bir Bakış".* Fe Dergi 7, No. 2, 2015, 48-58.

Valetas, Marie-France. *"The Name of Married Women in the European Union."* Populations et Sociétés 367, 2001: 1-4.

Van Booy, Simon. The Secret Lives of People in Love. Oneworld Publications, 2014.

Van Maanen, John. *Tales of the Field: On Writing Ethnography.* 2nd ed. Chicago Guides to Writing, Editing, and Publishing. Chicago: University of Chicago Press, 2011.

Vannini, Phillip. *"Ethnographic Film and Video on Hybrid Television: Learning from the Content, Style, and Distribution of Popular Ethnographic Documentaries."* Journal of Contemporary Ethnography 44, no. 4, 2015: 391-416.

Yaraman, Ayşegül-Başbuğu. *Elinin Hamuruyla Özgürlük.* Milliyet Yayınları, 1992.

Yaraman, Ayşegül. "Sorunları mı Sorumluluktan, Sorumluluğu mu Sorunlarından? Kadınlık Durumu, Kadınlık Bilinci ve Sevgi Soysal", S.Şahin, İ.Şahbenderoğlu (ed.) İsyankar Neşe / Sevgi Soysal Kitabı, İletişim Yayınları, İstanbul, 2015: 35-49.

Weiser, Eric B. *"#Me: Narcissism and its Facets as Predictors of Selfie-posting Frequency."* Personality and Individual Differences 86, 2015: 477-481.

Wilson, Rebekah. *"A Name of One's Own: Identity, Choice and Performance in Marital Relationships."* PhD diss., The London School of Economics and Political Science (LSE), 2009.

Zikopoulos, Paul, and Chris Eaton. *Understanding Big Data: Analytics for Enterprise Class Hadoop and Streaming Data.* McGraw-Hill Osborne Media, 2011.

Further Readings

Bachmann, Ingeborg. *Malina: A Novel.* Portico Paperbacks, 1999.

Eco, Umberto, Caterina Mongiat Farina, and Geoff Farina. *How to Write a Thesis.* Cambridge, Massachusetts: MIT Press, 2015.

Ellis, Carolyn, and Arthur P. Bochner, eds. *Composing Ethnography: Alternative Forms of Qualitative Writing.* Rowman Altamira, 1996.

Gandhi, Mahatma. *Autobiography: The Story of My Experiments with Truth.* Courier Corporation, 1983.

Janesick, Valerie J. *"The Dance of Qualitative Research Design: Metaphor, Methodolatry, and Meaning."* In N. K. Denzin and Y. S. Lincoln (Eds.), Handbook of Qualitative Research. Thousand Oaks, CA, US: Sage Publications, Inc. 1994: 209-219.

Muncey, Tessa. *Creating Autoethnographies.* Los Angeles; London: Sage, 2010.

Rabiger, Michael. *Directing the Documentary.* Focal Press, 2014.

Reinharz, Shulamit, and Lynn Davidman. *Feminist Methods in Social Research.* New York: Oxford University Press, 1992.

Robson, Colin. *Real World Research: A Resource for Social Scientists and Practitioner-Researchers.* 2nd ed. Oxford, UK; Madden, Mass: Blackwell Publishers, 2002.

Smith-Sullivan, Kendall. *"The Autoethnographic Call: Current Considerations and Possible Futures."* University of South Florida, 2008.

Soysal, Sevgi. *Tutkulu Perçem.* İletişim Yayıncılık, İstanbul. 2004.

Soysal, Sevgi. *Tante Rosa.* İletişim Yayıncılık, İstanbul, 2004.

Spry, Tami. *Body, Paper, Stage: Writing and Performing Autoethnography.* Qualitative Inquiry and Social Justice. Walnut Creek, Calif: Left Coast Press, Inc, 2011.

Filmography

Daguerréotypes, directed by Agnès Varda. (1976; France, INA, Film)

Daughter Rite, directed by Michele Citron. (1978; USA, Iris Films)

Kadının Adı Yok / The Woman Has No Name, directed by Atıf Yılmaz. [from a book by Duygu Asena] (1988; Turkey, Gala Film, DVD)

La Chambre, directed by Chantal Akerman. (1972; US: Paradise Films, DVD)

Mirror Mirror, directed by Zemirah Moffat. (2006; UK: University of Westminster, PhD Film)

Nana, Mom and Me, directed by Amalie Rothschild. (1974; New Jersey, New Day Films)

News from Home, directed by Chantal Akerman. (1977; The New York Films, DVD)

Rufus Stone, directed by Josh Appignanesi. [from a story by Kip Jones] (2012; UK: Parkville Pictures, Film)

Sex and the City, created by Darren Star. (1998-2004; USA, Darren Star Productions, TV Series)

Sybil, directed by Daniel Petrie. (1976; New York City, Warner Bros., DVD)

The Truman Show, directed by Peter Weir. (1998; US: Los Angeles, Film)

Uçurtmayı Vurmasınlar / Don't Let Them Shoot the Kite, directed by Tunç Başaran. [from a book by Feride Çiçekoğlu] (1989; Turkey, Magnum Film)

Uncle Yanco, directed by Agnès Varda. (1967; France, Film)

Yok Anasının Soyadı / Mrs His Name, directed by Hande Çayır. (2012; İstanbul, Turkey, Film)

Weekend, directed by Jean-Luc Godard. (1967; France, Athos Films, DVD)

Index

M

mainstream cinema, 45
marriage, xiii, xiv, xv, xx, 1, 2, 3, 5,
7, 10, 12, 26, 28, 30, 35, 36, 47,
65, 72, 73, 77
masculinity, 11
methodology, xvii, xviii, xix, 15, 16,
18, 21, 22, 41, 69, 79
Moffat Zemirah, xxi
Moroğlu Nazan, 5
Muhiddin Nezihe, 27
Mulvey Laura, 42
Mungan Murathan, 4

N

namelessness, 11
Neyzi Leyla, xviii
Nihal Şükûfe, 26
non-linear, 63

O

open-endedness, xxii, 53, 79
oral history, xviii, 41

P

Parks Rosa, 19
Parman Talat, 11
participatory culture, xix, xxi, 53,
54, 55, 64, 70, 77, 79
patriarchy, 2, 4, 78
personal is political, xix, xx, 1, 19
power, xix, xxi, 3, 4, 17, 31, 44, 50,
53, 64, 65, 66, 67, 70, 72, 77, 78
practice-led research, xxi
public sphere, 1
Purple Roof Women's Shelter
Foundation, vii, 29, 32, 33, 34

R

regime of truth, 11
representation, xiii, 19, 24, 34, 40,
43, 44, 50, 62, 65, 75
role models, 75
Rothschild Amalie, 45
Rouch Jean, 45

S

scat singing, 69, 71, 72
scientific research, xvii, 77
second sex, 34
secret password, 13
self, vii, xiii, xvii, xviii, xix, xxi, 3, 4,
10, 12, 15, 17, 18, 19, 20, 21, 22,
24, 33, 34, 36, 41, 43, 45, 47, 50,
60, 61, 63, 65, 66, 67, 70, 77, 78,
79
Selfie Age, 63, 64, 65, 66, 77, 78
Sexton Finck Larissa, xix
silenced voices, 22
Simone Nina, 72
slave, 38
social media, xxi, 53, 54, 63, 64, 66,
77
soulmate, xix
spreadability, 54, 55, 61, 79
Spry Tami, xviii, 69
stigma, 60
Stone Lucy, 36
subjectivity, xix, 16, 17, 18, 23, 24,
44, 70, 77, 78
surname, xiii, xiv, xv, xix, xx, 1, 2, 3,
4, 5, 6, 7, 8, 9, 10, 12, 13, 25, 26,
27, 28, 29, 30, 34, 35, 36, 37, 38,
40, 48, 49, 53, 57, 60, 65, 68, 72,
73, 74, 75, 76, 77

www.ingramcontent.com/pod-product-compliance
Lightning Source LLC
Chambersburg PA
CBHW062042270326
41929CB00014B/2513